FIVE AMERICAN POETS

MICHAEL SCHMIDT OBE FRSL is Professor of Poetry at the University of Glasgow. He is Editorial and Managing Director of Carcanet Press and general editor of *PN Review*. He is a poet, translator, literary critic and historian.

CLIVE WILMER was born in Harrogate in 1945, grew up in London and was educated at King's College, Cambridge. He now teaches English at Cambridge, where he is a Bye-Fellow of Fitzwilliam College and a Fellow of Sidney Sussex College. He has published five poetry collections with Carcanet, including *The Mystery of Things* (2006). He has edited the essays of Thom Gunn and Donald Davie and is a frequent contributor to the *Times Literary Supplement*, *PN Review* and other journals.

American poetry from Carcanet Press

John Ashbery
Djuna Barnes
Elizabeth Bishop
Lucie Brock-Broido
Robert Creeley
Hilda Doolittle (H.D.)
Louise Glück
Jorie Graham
Kelly Grovier
Marilyn Hacker
Edward Hirsch
Richard Howard
Laura (Riding) Jackson
Brigit Pegeen Kelly
Kenneth Koch
Mina Loy
Edna St Vincent Millay
Frank O'Hara
Charles Olson
Robert Rehder
Stephen Rodefer
James Schuyler
Arto Vaun
William Carlos Williams
Jane Yeh

Five American Poets

AN ANTHOLOGY

ROBERT HASS

JOHN MATTHIAS

JAMES MCMICHAEL

JOHN PECK

ROBERT PINSKY

Edited by
Michael Schmidt

With an introduction by
Clive Wilmer

CARCANET

First published in Great Britain in 2010 by
Carcanet Press Limited
Alliance House
Cross Street
Manchester M2 7AQ

Foreword copyright © Michael Schmidt 2010
Introduction copyright © Clive Wilmer 2010
Selections, biographical notes and afterwords © the individual poets

The right of Michael Schmidt, Clive Wilmer and of each poet
to be identified as the author of his work has been asserted by him
in accordance with the Copyright, Designs and Patents Act of 1988

Acknowledgements of permission to reprint in-copyright material
can be found on pp. 229–31 and constitute an extension of the copyright page.

A CIP catalogue record for this book is available from the British Library
ISBN 978 1 84777 070 7

The publisher acknowledges financial assistance from Arts Council England

Typeset in Bembo by XL Publishing Services, Tiverton
Printed and bound in England by SRP Ltd, Exeter

CONTENTS

ROBERT PINSKY

FOREWORD

When, in 1977, the idea for an anthology entitled *Five American Poets* occurred to me, I was reading an essay by John Matthias in *The New Review* in which he talked about Robert Pinsky's book *The Situation of Poetry*. It was an introduction for which I have remained grateful ever since. One thing that characterises these poets is that they write so illuminatingly about poetry, the art and the vocation, its place in history and in the present. Their concerns and voices have been different from the start and anything but static: the evolution of Pinsky and Hass as critics has contributed to the wider discourse on Anglophone and translated poetry, McMichael has written illuminatingly on Joyce, as has Peck on Pound and Matthias on David Jones. There is about their work a grateful sense of discovery and rediscovery. There is for each of them an inescapable civic dimension to the critical as to the poetic act, and a reluctance to allow poetry to retire into the comfortable shadows of the academy.

They also share a conviction that poetry is an art with a history. In that 1977 review Matthias quoted Pinsky: 'The cost to a contemporary of not sufficiently understanding his tradition will be conventionality and mannerism.' His – and her – tradition is not necessarily a common one: class, geography, European and other antecedents, personal circumstances, all contribute to the traditions on which the poet's individual integrity is founded. However, there are common threads as well, and honouring them is part of the poet's and the critic's vocation.

When a book called *Five American Poets* was published in 1979, the five poets, then in their thirties, were already exploring different areas, but they still had common points of departure, as Clive Wilmer describes in his introduction. To him and to Robert Wells I owe my introduction to Yvor Winters, who is obliquely celebrated here, as is Donald Davie, both men who had recognised and nurtured the five in different ways at Stanford. And it was Clive Wilmer who made me aware of this generation of poets in the first place.

Carcanet went on to publish individual collections by three of the five. In 1979 the press brought out John Peck's second book, *The Broken Blockhouse Wall*, and Carcanet has continued publishing his work even when, for a period, he had no American publisher. He is central to Carcanet's concerns with Modernism and its aftermaths and has been a key figure in the development of *PN Review*. A year later we published Robert Pinsky's wonderful essay poem *An Explanation of America*, previewed in the original anthology, and in 1996 *The Figured Wheel*, his Collected Poems, appeared. Pinsky, too, has been a key contributor to *PN Review*. In 1981 Carcanet published *Praise* by Robert Hass, a poet and critic whose work was important in the unfolding of our enterprise and whose friendly candour as a correspondent was of value to me as an editor. In 1978 we exchanged some long letters in which he astutely, and generously, suggested that 'the act of social imagination on which the claims of [*PN Review*] can, for the future, be based hasn't been made yet'.

This new anthology has given me the opportunity to renew acquaintance with the work of James McMichael, whose sense of scale and whose wonderful long lines had attracted me in the original book. And John Matthias, the begetter of that volume, is also the begetter of this one, having challenged me to revisit these five writers and their five *oeuvres* and to see how far they had travelled. He too has contributed down the years to *PN Review*, and his poetry has appeared from Anvil Press and Salt Publishing in handsome editions.

Echoing John Matthias, I wrote in 1979 about the 'sanity, flexibility, clarity' and 'coherence' of these writers. At the end of the confused 1970s they represented something of a tonic, reconnecting poetry with some of the disciplines it had lost sight of during the decade. Thirty years later I am not sure that those are the chief attributes that recommend their work today. Those four words are awfully earnest and Augustan, and though all five poets are serious in manner and matter, their tonal diversity, their good humour and wit, are also generally, and generously, in play.

They are inventive. They have read Pound and Auden, they devise prosodies which revive traditional resources and invalidate the merely conventional. Their poetry is capable of argument and epiphany; the epistle and the lyric coexist. The body of their work coheres, but not perhaps in quite the way I thought it did back then. The trajectory of each of them, thirty years on, is momentous, as this book makes clear in the selection that each poet has made of his own work: five writers of the same generation setting out on a common quest and finding their different ways. One measure of their poetry is how much history – and not only American history – it contains. These imaginations have been fully alive in their time and to their time. That is one of the many elements that make their work resonant and engaging.

Michael Schmidt
2010

INTRODUCTION

1

The title of this anthology repeats that of a book published thirty years ago. It had the same publisher as this one and included the same five poets. In 1979 the names of Robert Hass, John Matthias, James McMichael, John Peck and Robert Pinsky were new even to American readers. They will still be new to many British readers, though all of them now have substantial careers behind them – as this new book will show. In 1979, Michael Schmidt of Carcanet was not expecting to make a publishing sensation, but to back these five was to make a courageous statement about the future of American poetry and its descent from the great masters of the early twentieth century. For some of us, moreover, the book was a revelation. To speak personally, I cannot imagine how I would have developed without such poems as Hass's 'Meditation at Lagunitas', Matthias's 'Clarification for Robert Jacoby', McMichael's 'Itinerary', Peck's 'Cider and Vesalius' and Pinsky's 'Essay on Psychiatrists'. They enabled me to think about the world in the terms of my own era. And the *world* was what it was – not some distorting mirror of obsessive selfhood. This is to say, not that the self was absent from their poems – far from it – but that they cared about history and language.

I am not talking about a movement. What drew the five of them together was a common background: friendships that began in the mid-1960s, when they met at Stanford University, California, as students of Yvor Winters. That they have stayed in touch for more than forty years, and that the contact must have more to do with poetry than with the occurrences of daily life, is surely significant. Yet, if one looks at them superficially, they cannot as poets be said to have much in common. There is considerable difference between, say, Robert Pinsky, with his attachment to ordinary discourse, and John Matthias's neo-Modernism, allusive, discontinuous and textually self-conscious.

A similar contrast might be made between Robert Hass, with his quest for an accurate language of desire, and his fellow Californian James McMichael, who seems to have built a style on inhibition. Peck is, like Matthias, a neo–Modernist and, like Hass, a master of the crisp Far Eastern image. By profession a Jungian analyst, moreover, he is preoccupied with the mysterious inwardness of human life, yet he values the objective structures of language and poetry quite as much as Pinsky does. So even in as brief a summary as this, one can see that what the five of them do have in common turns out to be a great deal more than is at first apparent. In the context of cultural fragmentation, their wish to stay in touch – to communicate as poets across a large and complex country – implies involvement in some larger purpose. They have heeded the developments and disruptions of the later twentieth century, yet seem to share a need for a common culture. Behind them is this fundamental faith, tested to endurance by the politics of our era, that a common language implies a common society.

If what I suggest is so, we might wonder if it has anything to do with Winters's tutelage, for belief in a common language as the basis for social order and personal sanity lay at the heart of his teaching and example. Introducing the 1979 anthology, Michael Schmidt had this to say:

> One might be tempted to denominate them the 'last generation' of Wintersians, but this would be an error. To an extent they shared an apprenticeship, but they fell under the influence of the old man in different ways and to different extents, and as their work matured they moved beyond his influence and away from one another.

Schmidt went on to deduce that what they owed to Winters was 'as much a moral as a poetic debt':

> All five evince one element of Wintersian discipline – in Matthias's words, 'sanity at work in poetry even where emotion is nearly intolerable'. Sanity, flexibility, clarity, coherence: these are antique virtues, virtues which are very much at a premium in contemporary verse. The feelings and ideas of these five poets emerge through a world perceived as external and shared.

These are poets who have lived through an era which, as Matthias once put it, 'has seen important poetry published which is sometimes seriously unhinged or severely misshapen or obsessively violent'. It is not that they will not contemplate such disturbance. It is that they contemplate it in order to resist it.

2

Here is Robert Pinsky on Yvor Winters:

As to my own concerns, it seems odd, given
The ideas many of us have about art,
That so many writers, makers of films,

Artists, all suitors of excellence and their own
Genius, should consult psychiatrists, willing
To risk that the doctor in curing

The sickness should smooth away the cicatrice
Of genius, too. But it is all bosh, the false
Link between genius and sickness,

Except perhaps as they were linked
By the Old Man, addressing his class
On the first day: *"I know why you are here.*

You are here to laugh. You have heard of a crazy
Old man who believes that Robert Bridges
Was a good poet; who believes that Fulke

Greville was a great poet, greater than Philip
Sidney; who believes that Shakespeare's Sonnets
Are not all that they are cracked up to be... Well,

I will tell you something: I will tell you
What this course is about. Sometime in the middle
Of the Eighteenth Century, along with the rise

Of capitalism and scientific method, the logical
Foundations of Western thought decayed and fell apart.
When they fell apart, poets were left

With emotions and experiences, and with no way
To examine them. At this time, poets and men
Of genius began to go mad. Gray went mad. Collins

Went mad. Kit Smart was mad. William Blake surely
Was a madman. Coleridge was a drug addict, with severe
Depression. My friend Hart Crane died mad. My friend

Ezra Pound is mad. But you will not go mad; you will grow up
To become happy, sentimental old college professors,
Because they were men of genius, and you

Are not; and the ideas which were vital
To them are mere amusement to you. I will not
Go mad, because I have understood those ideas ...."

He drank wine and smoked his pipe more than he should;
In the end his doctors in order to prolong life
Were forced to cut away most of his tongue.

That was their business. As far as he was concerned
Suffering was life's penalty; wisdom armed one
Against madness; speech was temporary; poetry was truth.

Thom Gunn, who also studied under Winters and was second to none in his admiration for him, used to declare that the old man was 'too strong'; if a poet was to keep an identity, some distance from Winters was necessary. This section from Pinsky's 'An Essay on Psychiatrists' was included in the 1979 anthology. It is unmistakeably a tribute to Winters, but it is hedged with a reserve comparable to Gunn's. The italicised passage mimes the tone and vocabulary of Winters's criticism and presumably of his teaching. But it is bracketed within a larger context that renders it much more problematical than it would appear if confined to the 'quoted' words. It is significant that Pinsky's prosody, modelled on blank verse, departs much further from the norm than Winters would have found acceptable. It is as if the student, in the act of paying tribute to the master, were seeking simultaneously to flout him. Pinsky is probably closer to Winters than the other four in this book, but the careful measuring of distance in this extract may perhaps be taken as speaking for all of them. John Peck has also written an *hommage*. His poem 'The Upper Trace' – also included in 1979 – is an extended metaphor for his literary relationship with Winters. Peck's imagery and prosody owe a little to the master's early Imagist free verse. If I read the poem correctly, it pays homage to Winters, while announcing Peck's departure from the fold in the very language Winters had come to reject.

A handful of Winters's poems deserve to be placed among the greatest of the twentieth century, and it is a scandal that collections of record such as *The Norton Anthology* include not a single one of them. But much in his work has faded beyond revival. As Hass points out in an essay, Winters 'never solved for himself the problem of getting from image to discourse in the language of his time, and instead borrowed the solution of another age'. Though that is perhaps to overstate the case, it is true that stiffness of syntax and archaic diction render some of his poems almost unreadable. In the criticism, the problems are manifold. To instance a few: there is his authoritarian habit of announcing which lines in a poem are the good ones, his wilful narrowing of the canon, his dismissal of bodies of poetry outside his own experience, his tendency to applaud the products of his own classes above the more obvious stars of their generation. But there remains a striking body of good criticism in Winters's books as well as some acute and humane reflections on politics, society and cultural change. It is wrong to think of Winters as a conservative, though he undoubtedly had conserving instincts. In politics his convictions were radical – from his youthful socialism to the Rooseveltian liberalism of his prime. If he called himself a literary reactionary, that meant he had literally reacted against the advances made by Romanticism and Modernism. It had not been the reflex of an ageing man nostalgic for the past. On the contrary, Winters's early poetry is radically modern, indebted to Pound and Williams and H.D., and in his 'reactionary' work – especially in the couplet poems of the 1930s ('The Slow Pacific Swell', 'A View of Pasadena from the Hills', and so on) – he incorporates Modernist insights and procedures. His best poems are inconceivable without the innovations of the Symbolists and certain of their twentieth-century heirs. The difference is in the degree of control imposed on connotation and the unstated rational argument implied in the sequencing of imagery. Winters's mature poetry could not be called Modernist, but it cannot be understood outside a Modernist context.

It was in the poetry of Hart Crane that Winters most clearly identified the dangers of Modernism, as he saw them. His objection to Crane, whose poems he had loved as a young man, and for which he never lost his admiration, was that their oceanic emotions – the utter absorption in otherness expressed in their rhythms and imagery – would logically result in self-annihilation.

That Crane committed suicide, and that he did so, as if symbolically, by drowning himself in the ocean, seemed ample proof of the argument. The alternative position – the one which Winters followed in his work – was to limit the emotional power that poetry is able to attain. The emotion, Winters argued, should be appropriate to the experience and, for it to be so, the poet needs a rational discipline to order and control the means of expression. It is not the poet's business to submit to feeling, but to seek to appraise and understand the experiences that give rise to it.

It was this, rather than reactionary politics, that led Winters to advocate a return to traditional metres rigorously understood, and to a language that stands at a distance from experience. Such a view of language was philosophically realist rather than nominalist, nominalism seeming to Winters the curse of Modernism. If words, as Justinian said, are the consequences of things, then the basis of all language is denotation. Poetry is only another form of language, though one in which connotation and emotional resonance play an exceptional part. The great poet, according to Winters's doctrine, is always in control of connotation, and this – as our five poets plainly see – is a matter of continuing relevance.

3

In his book *In Defense of Reason* Winters writes: 'A poem is a statement in words about a human experience.' The key word there is 'about'. For Winters we write poems to reflect on our experiences, not to create autonomous art objects. Re-reading the first *Five American Poets* to seek out continuities with the present one, I have come to realise that Hass, McMichael, Matthias, Peck and Pinsky have all been profoundly touched by Winters's view, if only in some degree to react against it. That they have not followed his example is significant, but I am less struck by that than by the comparable reserve they have shown towards the orthodoxies of their own time, most of which began as rebellions. The five are roughly a decade younger than, say, Sylvia Plath, and therefore a decade older than her imitators. When still very young, they imbibed the work of Ginsberg and the Beats, but the effect of such poets on them was to prove minimal: it was more important to contemplate the possibility of poems made out of pure impulse, than to write such poems themselves.

They belong, that is to say, to the era of dissent and youthful rebellion, learning their art at a time of radical change. Born between 1939 and 1941, they were at Stanford during the war in Vietnam. The atmosphere of the period is still captured in the slogan 'Make love, not war'. The last years of the 1960s saw the eruption of the neo-Marxist critique of capitalism and the vision of a society transfigured by the liberating force of desire. This was of generative importance in the work of Hass and McMichael in particular, but it is there to a certain extent in all five. As things have turned out, and as this anthology shows, the energy of that era has abated, its implications for good and ill still not fully worked out. But the explosion of impulse, political, sexual and poetic, is at the centre of their work, even if in their different ways they have lost innocence and accepted other imperatives. In this context their relation to Winters is inescapably fraught with tensions. Winters was a liberal – actively engaged in the promotion of democracy and opposition to racism. But his humanist convictions, both political and poetic, assumed the need for order and containment. Such assumptions were not compatible with the freeing of the unconscious and the attack on bourgeois values. There is a nice irony in the fact that Winters's critique of Modernism was directed against its flirtations with fascism and that it was that very literary movement that attracted the experimental poets on the left.

The process is perhaps best traced in the work of James McMichael. McMichael began his career as a strict Wintersian, but his first book, published in 1971, reveals a poet newly drawn to the 'deep image' surrealism of Robert Bly and James Wright, a poetry that eschews rational discourse and objective form, opening itself to the force of unconscious impulse and suggestion. Within three years, however, McMichael had modified that stance. 'Itinerary' (1974), the first of the longer semi-narrative poems upon which his *oeuvre* is built, was to be among the highlights of the 1979 *Five American Poets*. Steeped in Wintersian images and notions, it maps out a relentlessly non-Wintersian course. Based on the records of the early nineteenth-century Lewis and Clark expedition across America, it evokes that journey as a metaphor for its own procedures. It becomes a journey into the unconscious of white America, the colonisation of a new country being equated with the conscious mind's suppression of the body and its desires. In its equation of 'earth' and 'body', the poem can now be understood, among other things, as an early contribution to environmentalism, a movement anticipated by Winters himself in several of his best poems (e.g., 'An Elegy: for the USN Dirigible, Macon'). McMichael has absorbed that aspect of Winters's thought but gives expression to it through Modernist and Postmodernist strategies. His subsequent semi-narratives – the extraordinary 'Four Good Things' and 'Each in a Place Apart' – apply similar procedures to his own life and background. They begin from Confessional assumptions but proceed in a manner that is anything but self-regarding.

The Confessional also finds a place in the work of John Matthias. He had been taught by John Berryman before he went to Stanford, and there were circumstances in his background that made some sort of analogy with Robert Lowell's *Life Studies* almost inevitable, a collection that was then, for anyone who cared about poetry, compulsory reading. But the intense self-absorption of Lowell's school is at odds with Matthias's main creative impulse. The key to Matthias, in fact, is a passion for that otherness in which we may see ourselves and our circumstances reflected. His interest in Britain is relevant here. He has lived in Britain for substantial periods and has an English wife, facts which one inevitably associates with his love of East Anglian landscape, English music, Old and Middle English as languages and English building in the Middle Ages. Of these five poets, he is the most committed to something like a continuation of Modernism, but he has been especially drawn to British versions of it – to Hugh MacDiarmid, Basil Bunting and, above all, David Jones, whose work he has introduced and edited. Matthias's route into Jones's peculiarly Latin and Anglo-Welsh version of Britain must have been by way of Ezra Pound, for Jones shares with Pound the urge to build a poem from documents, material residues and historical juxtapositions. There is in Matthias something of the historical materialist. That and his Modernism set him at odds with Winters, yet behind both in Matthias's practice is a belief – not at all alien to Winters – in the poet's responsibility to an objective world.

John Peck has written illuminatingly on Jones, Bunting and, above all, Ezra Pound. It is at the school of Pound and Bunting that his exceptional ear for the music of verse has been trained, but the Wintersian impress sank as deeply into Peck as into McMichael. As Donald Davie pointed out in a review of Peck's first book, the magnificent *Shagbark* of 1972, Peck brings complex syntax to Pound's 'ideogramic method' and writes a poetry resistant to fragmentation. Davie, who supervised Peck's Ph.D. dissertation on Pound, began the work of bringing the traditions of Pound and Winters back into communication, which Peck has continued. With his Jungian training, moreover, Peck is moved by the continuities and interactions between, on the one hand, history and the physical world and, on the other, the interior life of 'memories, dreams and reflections'. His work insists on the connections between the collective unconscious and the objective presence of human artefacts. If Peck retains some loyalty towards the humanist account of rationality expressed by Winters, he is also conscious of other sorts of wisdom that come from the deeper reaches of the mind. For a magisterial example, see the brief lyric 'He who called blood builder' (p. 138), which draws, *inter alia*, on Mandelstam and on Virgil's *Aeneid*.

The poet least affected by Winters is, on the face of it, Robert Hass, who was obviously more impressed in his student days by the Beat Generation and experiments with Japanese haiku. Like Gary Snyder, whom he admired early on, Hass seems in his early work to have little to do with the traditions of English at all. Like Snyder, he is interested in the simple process of naming: in the power of words to suggest the vulnerable specifics of our exis-tence – the sensuous particulars of the world, the natural circumstances of shared lives. Almost inevitably, though, he then reflects on the relation of word to thing, suggesting that perhaps, in the act of naming, we only succeed in distancing the world. Thus, despite the sensuous immediacy of his work, Hass involves himself and his readers in the problems of Postmodernity. What he says about naming, moreover, has relevance to environmental issues. It is significant that he has become the most prominent of the translators of the great Polish poet Czesław Miłosz, who was troubled by what he saw as the dangerous innocence of American attitudes to nature.

Robert Pinsky has also translated Miłosz, and might have been thought the more obvious candidate for the job. His career has been like Hass's in reverse. He has something of the public poet about him. In many of his poems, he reflects in a confidently civilised manner on the issues of the day, as if (unusually for a modern poet) he had a large public in mind. He is the author of a discursive book-length poem, *An Explanation of America*, and the present selection includes his reflections on that core symbol of mass communication in Postmodern societies, the TV set. If the risk for Hass was that he might have become the naive celebrator of our bond with the natural world, the risk for Pinsky would be that of becoming too smoothly communicative. But as we have seen with 'An Essay on Psychiatrists', the matter is much more complex. It is significant that the most impressive of his later poems is an *ode* (in an era sceptical of classical genres) to *meaning* (that aspect of language most fiercely interrogated by Postmodernists). Yet the element of playful reflexiveness in the poem might itself be understood as Postmodern. From a Wintersian point of view, Pinsky's position is the most fascinating. Of the five poets in this book, he is most nearly at ease with Winters's outlook, yet from first to last he frames that outlook with questions.

4

I myself was affected by Yvor Winters, originally as a result of his impact on British poets – on Donald Davie, Thom Gunn, Dick Davis and Robert Wells. As a result, I went on to acquaint myself with Winters's students and followers. When Hass and Matthias came to Cambridge (where I live) as Visiting Scholars in the 1970s, I got to know them, and it was largely through Matthias that I first discovered McMichael, Peck, and Pinsky. I remember Matthias saying to me one day that, though their three friends had been influenced by Winters, neither he nor Hass had ever been tempted along that route. I am not sure he would be as categorical today, and even then he almost immediately conceded that all of them had absorbed the issues that Winters had raised and continued in their work to deal with them. That is how true poetry works, of course: it is a sort of conversation – often a conversation across history, always a conversation with friends, rivals and teachers.

Clive Wilmer
Cambridge 2009

Five American Poets

ROBERT HASS

Robert Hass was born in San Francisco, California and lives across the bay in Berkeley where he is a professor at the University of California. He is the author of six books of poetry and a volume of essays, *Twentieth Century Pleasures* (1984). For four years he wrote a weekly poetry column for the *Washington Post*. These columns have been collected in two volumes, *Poet's Choice: Poems for Everyday Life* (1999) and *Now and Then: The Poet's Choice Columns 1997–99* (2006). He has published a volume of translations of the classic Japanese haiku poets, *The Essential Haiku: Versions of Bashō, Buson, and Issa*, and translated with the author many volumes of the poetry of Czesław Miłosz. Between 1976 and 1977 he lived in Little Shelford in Cambridgeshire as a fellow of the US-UK Bicentennial Exchange Program, and he has been a Samuel Fischer Guest Professor at the Free University in Berlin. He is twice a winner of the National Book Critics Circle Award, once in poetry and once in criticism. *Time and Materials*, published in 2007, won both the National Book Award and the Pulitzer Prize.

Heroic Simile

When the swordsman fell in Kurosawa's *Seven Samurai*
in the gray rain,
in Cinemascope and the Tokugawa dynasty,
he fell straight as a pine, he fell
as Ajax fell in Homer
in chanted dactyls and the tree was so huge
the woodsman returned for two days
to that lucky place before he was done with the sawing
and on the third day he brought his uncle.

They stacked logs in the resinous air,
hacking the small limbs off,
tying those bundles separately.
The slabs near the root
were quartered and still they were awkwardly large;
the logs from midtree they halved:
ten bundles and four great piles of fragrant wood,
moons and quarter moons and half moons
ridged by the saw's tooth.

The woodsman and the old man his uncle
are standing in midforest
on a floor of pine silt and spring mud.
They have stopped working
because they are tired and because
I have imagined no pack animal
or primitive wagon. They are too canny
to call in neighbors and come home
with a few logs after three days' work.
They are waiting for me to do something
or for the overseer of the Great Lord
to come and arrest them.

How patient they are!
The old man smokes a pipe and spits.
The young man is thinking he would be rich
if he were already rich and had a mule.

Ten days of hauling
and on the seventh day they'll probably
be caught, go home empty-handed
or worse. I don't know
whether they're Japanese or Mycenaean
and there's nothing I can do.
The path from here to that village
is not translated. A hero, dying,
gives off stillness to the air.
A man and a woman walk from the movies
to the house in the silence of separate fidelities.
There are limits to imaginaton.

Meditation at Lagunitas

All the new thinking is about loss.
In this it resembles all the old thinking.
The idea, for example, that each particular erases
the luminous clarity of a general idea. That the clown-
faced woodpecker probing the dead sculpted trunk
of that black birch is, by his presence,
some tragic falling off from a first world
of undivided light. Or the other notion that,
because there is in this world nó one thing
to which the bramble of *blackberry* corresponds,
a word is elegy to what it signifies.
We talked about it late last night and in the voice
of my friend, there was a thin wire of grief, a tone
almost querulous. After a while 1 understood that,
talking this way, everything dissolves: *justice,*
pine, hair, woman, you and *I.* There was a woman
I made love to and I remembered how, holding
her small shoulders in my hands sometimes,
I felt a violent wonder at her presence
like a thirst for salt, for my childhood river
with its island willows, silly music from the pleasure boat,
muddy places where we caught the little orange-silver fish

called *pumpkinseed*. It hardly had to do with her.
Longing, we say, because desire is full
of endless distances. I must have been the same to her.
But I remember so much, the way her hands dismantled bread,
the thing her father said that hurt her, what
she dreamed. There are moments when the body is as numinous
as words, days that are the good flesh continuing.
Such tenderness, those afternoons and evenings,
saying *blackberry, blackberry, blackberry.*

The Yellow Bicycle

The woman I love is greedy,
but she refuses greed.
She walks so straightly.
When I ask her what she wants,
she says, "A yellow bicycle."

★

Sun, sunflower,
coltsfoot on the roadside,
a goldfinch, the sign
that says Yield, her hair,
cat's eyes, his hunger
and a yellow bicycle.

★

Once, when they had made love in the middle of the night and it
was very sweet, they decided they were hungry, so they got up,
got dressed, and drove downtown to an all-night donut shop.
Chicano kids lounged outside, a few drunks, and one black man
selling dope. Just at the entrance there was an old woman in a
thin floral print dress. She was barefoot. Her face was covered
with sores and dry peeling skin. The sores looked like raisins and
her skin was the dry yellow of a parchment lampshade ravaged by

light and tossed away. They thought she must have been hungry
and, coming out again with a white paper bag full of hot rolls,
they stopped to offer her one. She looked at them out of her
small eyes, bewildered, and shook her head for a little while, and
said very kindly, "No."

★

Her song to the yellow bicycle:
The boats on the bay
have nothing on you,
my swan, my sleek one!

The Origin of Cities

She is first seen dancing which is a figure
not for art or prayer or the arousal of desire
but for action simply; her breastband is copper,
her crown imitates the city walls. Though she draws us
to her, like a harbor or a rivermouth she sends us away.
A figure of the outward. So the old men grown lazy
in patrician ways lay out cash for adventures.
Imagining a rich return, they buy futures
and their slaves haunt the waterfront for news of ships.
The young come from the villages dreaming.
Pleasure and power draw them. They are employed
to make inventories and grow very clever,
multiplying in their heads, deft at the use of letters.
When they are bored, they write down old songs from the villages,
and the cleverest make new songs in the old forms
describing the pleasures of the city, their mistresses,
old shepherds and simpler times. And the temple
where the farmer grandfathers of the great merchants worshipped,
the dim temple across from the marketplace
which was once a stone altar in a clearing in the forest,
where the nightwatch pisses now against a column in the moonlight,
is holy to them; the wheat mother their goddess of sweaty sheets,

of what is left in the air when that glimpsed beauty
turns the corner, of love's punishment and the wracking
of desire. They make songs about that. They tell
stories of heroes and brilliant lust among the gods.
These are amusements. She dances, the ships go forth,
slaves and peasants labor in the fields, maimed soldiers
ape monkeys for coins outside the wineshops,
the craftsmen work in bronze and gold, accounts
are kept carefully, what goes out, what returns.

The Beginning of September

I

The child is looking in the mirror.
His head falls to one side, his shoulders slump.
He is practicing sadness.

II

He didn't think she ought to
and she thought she should.

III

In the summer
peaches the color of sunrise

In the fall
plums the color of dusk

IV

Each thing moves its own way
in the wind. Bamboo flickers,
the plum tree waves, and the loquat
is shaken.

V

The dangers are everywhere. Auxiliary verbs, fishbones, a fine
carelessness. No one really likes the odor of geraniums, not the
woman who dreams of sunlight and is always late for work nor
the man who would be happy in altered circumstances. Words
are abstract, but *words are abstract* is a dance, car crash, heart's
delight. It's the design dumb hunger has upon the world.
Nothing is severed on hot mornings when the deer nibble flow-
erheads in a simmer of bay leaves. Somewhere in the summer
dusk is the sound of children setting the table. That is mastery:
spoon, knife, folded napkin, fork; glasses all around. The place for
the plate is wholly imagined. Mother sits here and father sits there
and this is your place and this is mine. A good story compels you
like sexual hunger but the pace is more leisurely. And there are
always melons.

VI

little mother
little dragonfly quickness of summer mornings
this is a prayer
this is the body dressed in its own warmth
at the change of seasons

VII

There are not always melons
There are always stories

Five American Poets

VIII

Chester found a dozen copies of his first novel in a used book-store and took them to the counter. The owner said, "You can't have them all," so Chester kept five. The owner said, "That'll be a hundred and twelve dollars." Chester said, "What?" and the guy said, "They're first editions, mac, twenty bucks apiece." And so Chester said, "Why are you charging me a hundred and twelve dollars?" The guy said, "Three of them are autographed." Chester said, "Look, I wrote this book." The guy said, "All right, a hundred. I won't charge you for the autographs."

IX

The insides of peaches
are the color of sunrise

The outsides of plums
are the color of dusk

X

Here are some things to pray to in San Francisco: the bay, the mountain, the goddess of the city; remembering, forgetting, sudden pleasure, loss; sunrise and sunset; salt; the tutelary gods of Chinese, Japanese, Russian, Basque, French, Italian and Mexican cooking; the solitude of coffee houses and museums; the virgin, mother and widow moons; hilliness, vistas; John McLaren; Saint Francis; the Mother of Sorrows; the rhythm of any life still whole through three generations; wine, especially zinfandel because from that Hungarian vine-slip came first a native wine not resinous and sugar-heavy; the sourdough mother, yeast and beginning; all fish and fisherman at the turning of the tide; the turning of the tide; eelgrass, oldest inhabitant; fog; seagulls; Joseph Worcester; plum blossoms; warm days in January…

XI

She thought it was a good idea.
He had his doubts.

XII

ripe blackberries

XIII

She said: reside, reside
and he said, gored heart
She said: sunlight, cypress
he said, idiot children
nibbling arsenic in flaking paint
she said: a small pool of semen
translucent on my belly
he said maybe he said
maybe

XIV

the sayings of my grandmother:
they're the kind of people
who let blackberries rot on the vine

XV

The child approaches the mirror very fast
then stops
and watches himself
gravely.

So summer gives over—
white to the color of straw
dove gray to slate blue
    burnishings
a little rain
a little light on the water

Privilege of Being

Many are making love. Up above, the angels
in the unshaken ether and crystal of human longing
are braiding one another's hair, which is strawberry blond
and the texture of cold rivers. They glance
down from time to time at the awkward ecstasy—
it must look to them like featherless birds
splashing in the spring puddle of a bed—
and then one woman, she is about to come,
peels back the man's shut eyelids and says,
look at me, and he does. Or is it the man
tugging the curtain rope in that dark theater?
Anyway, they do, they look at each other;
two beings with evolved eyes, rapacious,
startled, connected at the belly in an unbelievably sweet
lubricious glue, stare at each other,
and the angels are desolate. They hate it. They shudder pathetically
like lithographs of Victorian beggars
with perfect features and alabaster skin hawking rags
in the lewd alleys of the novel.
All of creation is offended by this distress.
It is like the keening sound the moon makes sometimes,
rising. The lovers especially cannot bear it,
it fills them with unspeakable sadness, so that
they close their eyes again and hold each other, each
feeling the mortal singularity of the body
they have enchanted out of death for an hour or so,

and one day, running at sunset, the woman says to the man,
I woke up feeling so sad this morning because I realized
that you could not, as much as I love you,
dear heart, cure my loneliness,
wherewith she touched his cheek to reassure him
that she did not mean to hurt him with this truth.
And the man is not hurt exactly,
he understands that life has limits, that people
die young, fail at love,
fail of their ambitions. He runs beside her, he thinks
of the sadness they have gasped and crooned their way out of
coming, clutching each other with old, invented
forms of grace and clumsy gratitude, ready
to be alone again, or dissatisfied, or merely
companionable like the couples on the summer beach
reading magazine articles about intimacy between the sexes
to themselves, and to each other,
and to the immense, illiterate, consoling angels.

Churchyard

Somerset Maugham said a professional was someone who could
do his best work when he didn't particularly feel like it. There
was a picture of him in the paper, a face lined deeply and morally
like Auden's, an old embittered tortoise, the corners of the mouth
turned down resolutely to express the idea that everything in life
is small change. And what he said when he died: I'm all through,
the clever young men don't write essays about me. In the fleshly
world, the red tulip in the garden sunlight is almost touched by
shadow and begins to close up. Someone asked me yesterday: are
deer monogamous? I thought of something I had read. When
deer in the British Isles were forced to live in the open because of
heavy foresting, it stunted them. The red deer who lived in the
Scottish highlands a thousand years ago were a third larger than
the present animal. This morning, walking into the village to pick
up the car, I thought of a roof where I have slept in the summer
in New York, pigeons in the early morning sailing up Fifth

Avenue and silence in which you imagine the empty canyons the light hasn't reached yet. I was standing on the high street in Shelford, outside the fussy little teashop, and I thought a poem with the quick, lice-ridden pigeons in it might end: this is a dawn song in Manhattan. I hurried home to write it and, as I passed the churchyard, school was letting out. Luke was walking toward me smiling. He thought I had come to meet him. That was when I remembered the car, when he was walking toward me through the spring flowers and the eighteenth-century gravestones, his arms full of school drawings he hoped not to drop in the mud.

Conversion

Walking down the stairs this morning in the bitter cold, in the old house's salt smell of decay, past the Mansergh family coat of arms on the landing, I longed for California and thought I smelled laurel leaves: riding an acacia limb in the spring, rivers of yellow pollen, wild fennel we broke into six-inch lengths and threw at each other in the neighborhood wars or crouched in thickets of broom, shooting blue jays with BB guns. *Oiseaux*, I read last week when I picked up a volume of Ponge in the bookshop on rue Racine and thought of blue jays and so bought the Ponge, thinking I would write grave, luminous meditative poems. And walking across the bridge later past Notre Dame, I remembered Jack Kjellen who lived with his mother the telephone operator and who always wanted to pretend that we were the children of Fatima having a vision of the Virgin, and I would have to go along for a while, hoping to lure him hack to playing pirates. Vision of Jack kneeling under the fig tree, palms prayerfully touching, looking up awed and reverent into the branches where the fat green figs hung like so many scrotums among the leaves. Scrota? But they were less differentiated than that: breasts, bottoms. The sexual ambiguity of flowers and fruits in French botanical drawings. Oh yes, sweet hermaphrodite peaches and the glister of plums!

Human Wishes

This morning the sun rose over the garden wall and a rare blue sky leaped from east to west. Man is altogether desire, say the Upanishads. Worth anything, a blue sky, says Mr. Acker, the Shelford gardener. Not altogether. In the end. Last night on television the ethnologist and the cameraman watched with hushed wonder while the chimpanzee carefully stripped a willow branch and inserted it into the anthill. He desired red ants. When they crawled slowly up the branch, he ate them, pinched between long fingers as the zoom lens enlarged his face. Sometimes he stopped to examine one, as if he were a judge at an ant beauty contest or God puzzled suddenly by the idea of suffering. There was an empty place in the universe where that branch wasn't and the chimp filled it, as Earlene, finding no back on an old Welsh cupboard she had bought in Saffron Walden, imagined one there and imagined both the cupboard and the imagined back against a kitchen wall in Berkeley, and went into town looking for a few boards of eighteenth-century tongue and groove pine to fill that empty space. I stayed home to write, or rather stayed home and stared at a blank piece of paper, waiting for her to come back, thinking tongue and groove, tongue and groove, as if language were a kind of moral cloud chamber through which the world passed and from which it emerged charged with desire. The man in the shop in Cambridge said he didn't have any old pine, but when Earlene went back after thinking about it to say she was sure she had seen some, the man found it. Right under his feet, which was puzzling. Mr. Acker, hearing the story, explained. You know, he said, a lot of fiddling goes on in those places. The first time you went in, the governor was there, the second time he wasn't, so the chap sold you some scrap and he's four quid in pocket. No doubt he's having a good time now with his mates in the pub. Or he might have put it on the horses at Newmarket. He might parley it into a fortune.

The Apple Trees at Olema

They are walking in the woods along the coast
and in a grassy meadow, wasting, they come upon
two old neglected apple trees. Moss thickened
every bough and the wood of the limbs looked rotten
but the trees were wild with blossom and a green fire
of small new leaves flickered even on the deadest branches.
Blue-eyes, poppies, a scattering of lupine,
flecked the meadow, and an intricate, leopard-spotted
leaf-green flower whose name they didn't know.
Trout lily, he said; she said, adder's-tongue.
She is shaken by the raw, white, backlit flaring
of the apple blossoms. He is exultant,
as if some thing he felt were verified,
and looks to her to mirror his response.
If it is afternoon, a thin moon of my own dismay
fades like a scar in the sky to the east of them.
He could be knocking wildly at a closed door
in a dream. She thinks, meanwhile, that moss
resembles seaweed drying lightly on a dock.
Torn flesh, it was the repetitive torn flesh
of appetite in the cold white blossoms
that had startled her. Now they seem tender
and where she was repelled she takes the measure
of the trees and lets them in. But he no longer
has the apple trees. This is as sad or happy
as the tide, going out or coming in, at sunset.
The light catching in the spray that spumes up
on the reef is the color of the lesser finch
they notice now flashing dull gold in the light
above the field. They admire the bird together,
it draws them closer, and they start to walk again.
A small boy wanders corridors of a hotel that way.
Behind one door, a maid. Behind another one, a man
in striped pajamas shaving. He holds the number
of his room close to the center of his mind
gravely and delicately, as if it were the key,
and then he wanders among strangers all he wants.

Misery and Splendor

Summoned by conscious recollection, she
would be smiling, they might be in a kitchen talking,
before or after dinner. But they are in this other room,
the window has many small panes, and they are on a couch
embracing. He holds her as tightly
as he can, she buries herself in his body.
Morning, maybe it is evening, light
is flowing through the room. Outside,
the day is slowly succeeded by night,
succeeded by day. The process wobbles wildly
and accelerates: weeks, months, years. The light in the room
does not change, so it is plain what is happening.
They are trying to become one creature,
and something will not have it. They are tender
with each other, afraid
their brief, sharp cries will reconcile them to the moment
when they fall away again. So they rub against each other,
their mouths dry, then wet, then dry.
They feel themselves at the center of a powerful
and baffled will. They feel
they are an almost animal,
washed up on the shore of a world—
or huddled against the gate of a garden—
to which they can't admit they can never be admitted.

Cuttings

Body Through Which the Dream Flows

You count up everything you have
or have let go.
What's left is the lost and the possible.
To the lost, the irretrievable
or just out of reach, you say:
light loved the pier, the seedy
string quartet of the sun going down over water
that gilds ants and beach fleas
ecstatic and communal on the stiffened body
of a dead grebe washed ashore
by last night's storm. Idiot sorrow,
an irregular splendor, is the half-sister
of these considerations.
To the possible you say nothing.
October on the planet.
Huge moon, bright stars.

The Lovers Undressing

They put on rising, and they rose.
They put on falling, and they fell.
They were the long grass on the hillside
that shudders in the wind. They sleep.
Days, kitchens. Cut flowers,
shed petals, smell of lemon, smell of toast
or soap. Are you upset about something,
one says. No, the other says.
Are you sure, the one says.
Yes, the other says, I'm sure.

Sad

Often we are sad animals.
Bored dogs, monkeys getting rained on.

Migration

A small brown wren in the tangle
of the climbing rose. April:
last rain, the first dazzle
and reluctance of the light.

Dark

Desire lies down with the day
and the night birds wake
to their fast heartbeats
in the trees. The woman beside you
is breathing evenly. All day
you were in a body. Now
you are in a skull. Wind,
streetlights, trees flicker
on the ceiling in the dark.

Things Change

Small song,
two beat:
the robin on the lawn
hops from sun
into shadow, shadow
into sun.

Stories in Bed

In the field behind her house, she said,
fennel grew high and green
in early summer, and the air
smelled like little anise-scented loaves
in the Italian restaurants her father
used to take them to on Sunday nights.
She had to sit up straight:
it was the idea of family
they failed at. She lights a cigarette,
remembering the taut veins
in her mother's neck, how she had studied them,
repelled. He has begun to drowse:
backyards, her voice, dusty fennel,
the festering sweetness of the plums.

Monday Morning, Late Summer

On the fence
in the sunlight,
beach towels.

No wind.

The apricots have ripened
and been picked.
The blackberries have ripened
and been picked.

So

They walked along the dry gully.
Cottonwoods, so the river must be underground.

Plus Which

She turned to him. Or, alternatively,
she turned away. Doves let loose
above the sea, or the sea at night
beating on the pylons of a bridge.
Off-season: the candles were mediterranean,
opaque, and the cat cried *olor*,
olor, *olor* in the blue susurrations
of heather by the outhouse door.

Santa Barbara Road

Mornings on the south side of the house
just outside the kitchen door
arrived early in summer—
when Luke was four or five
he would go out there, still in his dandelion-
yellow pajamas on May mornings
and lie down on the first warm stone.

For years, when the green nubs of apricots
first sprouted on the backyard tree,
I thought about a bench in that spot,
a redwood screen behind green brushstrokes
of bamboo, and one April, walking into the kitchen,
I felt like a stranger to my life
and it scared me, so when the gray doves returned
to the telephone wires
and the lemons were yellowing
and no other task presented itself,
I finally went into the garden and started
digging, trying to marry myself
and my hands to that place.

★

Five American Poets

Household verses: "Who are you?"
the rubber duck in my hand asked Kristin
once, while she was bathing, three years old.
"Kristin," she said, laughing, her delicious
name, delicious self. "That's just your name,"
the duck said. "Who are you?" "Kristin,"
she said. "Kristin's a name. Who are you?"
the duck asked. She said, shrugging,
"Mommy, Daddy, Leif."

★

The valley behind the hills heats up,
vultures, red-tailed hawks floating in the bubbles
of warm air that pull the fog right in
from the ocean. You have to rise at sunup
to see it steaming through the Gate
in ghostly June. Later, on street corners,
you can hardly see the children, chirping
and shivering, each shrill voice climbing over
the next in an ascending chorus. "Wait, you guys,"
one little girl says, trying to be heard.
"Wait, wait, wait, wait, wait."
Bright clothes: the last buses of the term.

★

Richard arrives to read poems, the final guest
of a long spring. I thought of Little Shelford,
where we had seen him last. In the worked gold
of an English October, Kristin watched the neighbor's
horses wading in the meadowgrass, while Leif
and I spiraled a football by the chalk-green,
moss-mortared ruin of the garden wall.
Mr. Acker, who had worked in the village
since he was a boy, touched his tweed cap
mournfully. "Reminds me of the war," he said.
"Lots of Yanks here then." Richard rolled a ball
to Luke, who had an old alphabet book
in which cherubic animals disported.

Richard was a *rabbit* with a *roller.*
Luke evidently thought that it was droll
or magical that Richard, commanded
by the power of the word, was crouching
under the horse-chestnut, dangling
a hand-rolled cigarette and rolling him a ball.
He gave me secret, signifying winks, though
he could not quite close one eye at a time.
So many prisms to construct a moment!
Spiderwebs set at all angles on a hedge:
what Luke thought was going on, what Mr. Acker
saw, and Richard, who had recently divorced,
idly rolling a ball with someone else's child,
healing slowly, as the neighbor's silky mare
who had had a hard birth in the early spring,
stood quiet in the field as May grew sweet,
her torn vagina healing. So many visions
intersecting at what we call the crystal
of a common world, all the growing and shearing,
all the violent breaks. On Richard's last night
in Berkeley, we drank late and drove home
through the city gardens in the hills. Light
glimmered on the bay. Night-blooming jasmine
gave a heavy fragrance to the air Richard
studied the moonlit azaleas in silence.
I knew he had a flat in East London.
I wondered if he was envying my life.
"How did you ever get stuck in this nest
of gentlefolk?" he said. "Christ! It's lovely.
I shouldn't want to live in America.
I'd miss the despair of European men."

★

Luke comes running in the house excited
to say that an Iceland poppy has "bloomed up."
His parents, who are not getting along
especially well, exchange wry looks.
They had both forgotten, since small children
were supposed to love flowers, that they actually

do. And there is the pathos of the metaphor
or myth: irresistible flowering.

★

Everything rises from the dead in June.
There is some treasure hidden in the heart of summer
everyone remembers now, and they can't be sure
the lives they live in will discover it.
They remember the smells of childhood vacations.
The men buy maps, raffish hats. Some women
pray to it by wearing blouses
with small buttons you have to button patiently
as if to say, this is not winter, not
the cold shudder of dressing in the dark.

★

Howard, one child on his shoulder,
another trotting beside him, small hand
in his hand, is going to write a book—
"Miranda, stop pulling Daddy's hair"—about
the invention of the family in medieval France.
The ritual hikes of Memorial Day: adults
chatting in constantly re-forming groups,
men with men, women with women, couples,
children cozened along with orange sections
and with raisins, running ahead, and back,
and interrupting. Long views through mist
of the scaly brightness of the ocean,
the massive palisade of Point Reyes cliffs.
"I would have thought," a woman friend says,
peeling a tangerine for Howard whose hands
are otherwise employed, cautioning a child
to spit out all the seeds, "that biology
invented the family." A sudden upward turn
of the trail, islands just on the horizon,
blue. "Well," he says, "I think it's useful
to see it as a set of conventions."

Someone's great-aunt dies. Someone's sister's
getting married in a week. The details are comic.
But we dress, play flutes, twine flowers,
and read long swatches from the Song of Songs
to celebrate some subtle alteration
in a cohabitation that has, probably, reached a crisis
and solved it with the old idea of these vows.
To vow, and tear down time: one of the lovers gives up
an apartment, returned to and stripped piecemeal
over months or years, until one maidenhair fern
left by the kitchen window as a symbol, dwindling,
of the resilience of a solitary life
required watering. Now it too is moved.

*

Summer solstice: parents, if their children
are young enough, put them to bed before dark,
then sit to watch the sun set on the bay.
A woman brings her coffee to the view.
Dinner done. What was she thinking
before her mother called, before the neighbor
called about the car pool? Something,
something interesting. The fog flares
and smolders, salmon first, then rose,
and in the twilight the sound comes up
across the neighborhood backyards of a table
being set. Other lives with other schedules.
Then dark, and, veering eerily, a bat.

*

Body half-emerged from the bright blue cocoon
of the sleeping bag, he wakes, curled hand
curling toward the waves of his sisters
cut-short, slept-on and matted, cornfield-
colored hair. She stirs a little in her sleep.
Her mother, whose curved brow her brow exactly

echoes, stirs. What if the gnostics had it backward?
What if eternity is pure destruction? The child,
rubbing his eyes, stares drowsily at the sea,
squints at his father who is sitting up,
shivers from his bag, plods up the beach
to pee against the cliff, runs back, climbs in
with his mother, wriggles close. In a minute
he'll be up again, fetching driftwood for a fire.

★

Leif comes home from the last day of his sophomore year.
I am sitting on the stoop by our half-dug,
still-imagined kitchen porch, reading
Han Dynasty rhyme-prose. He puts a hand on my shoulder,
grown to exactly my height and still growing.
"Dad," he says, "I'm not taking any more
of this tyrannical bullshit." I read to him
from Chia Ya: *The great man is without bent,*
a million changes are as one to him.
He says: "And another thing, don't lay
your Buddhist trips on me." *The span of life is fated;*
man cannot guess its ending.
In stillness like the stillness of deep springs...
In the kitchen he flips the lid
of the blueberry yogurt. I am thinking
this project is more work than I want.
Joining, scattering, ebbing and flowing,
where is there persistence, where is there rule?
"Bullshit," he mutters, "what is the existential reality"—
he has just read *Nausea* in advanced English—
"of all this bullshit, Todo?"
Todo is the dog. It occurs to me
that I am not a very satisfying parent
to rebel against. *Like an unmoored boat*
drifting aimlessly, not even valuing
the breath of life, the wise man
embraces nothing, and drifts with it.

I look at his long body in a chair
and wonder if I'd tell him to embrace the void.
I think he will embrace a lover soon.
I want the stars to terrify him once. I want him
to weep bitterly when his grandfather dies,
hating the floral carpet, hating it that his old aunts
have made the arrangements with such expertise.
I would ward off, if I could, the thicket
of grief on grief in which Chia Ya
came to entire relinquishment as to a clearing.
Digging again, I say, "You know, I started this job
and I hate it already, and now I have to finish."
He leans against the doorpost with a spoon.
Takes a mouthful. "Well, Pop," he says, "that's life."

                              *

Children stroll down to the lakeside
on a path already hot from the morning sun
and known well by them in its three turnings—
one by the sugar pine gouged with rusty nails
where summers past they put a hammock or a swing,
one by the thimbleberry where the walk seems driest,
dust heaviest on the broad soft leaves, and bees—
you have to be careful—are nuzzling in the flowers,
one by the aspens where the smell of water
starts and the path opens onto sand, the wide blue lake,
mountains on the farther shore. The smaller boy
has line, a can for crawfish, and an inner tube.
He's nursing a summer cold. His older brother's
carrying a book, a towel, a paper on *Medea*
his girlfriend has mailed to him from summer school.
The girl has several books, some magazines.
She loves her family, but she's bored. She'd rather
be in town where her friends are, where her real life
has begun. They settle on the beach.
Cold water, hot sun, the whole of an afternoon.

Like Three Fair Branches from One Root Deriv'd

I am outside a door and inside
the words do not fumble
as I fumble saying this.
It is the same in the dream
where I touch you. Notice
in this poem the thinning out
of particulars. The gate
with the three snakes is burning,
symbolically, which doesn't mean
the flames can't hurt you.
Now it is the pubic arch instead
and smells of oils and driftwood,
of our bodies working very hard
at pleasure but they are not
thinking about us. Bless them,
it is not a small thing to be
happily occupied, go by them
on tiptoe. Now the gate is marble
and the snakes are graces.
You are the figure in the center.
On the left you are going away
from yourself. On the right
you are coming back. Meanwhile
we are passing through the gate
with everything we love. We go
as fire, as flesh, as marble.
Sometimes it is good and sometimes
it is dangerous like the ignorance
of particulars, but our words are clear
and our movements give off light.

Robert Hass

Transparent Garments

Because it is neither easy nor difficult,
because the outer dark is not passport
nor is the inner dark, the horror
held in memory as talisman. Not to go in
stupidly holding out dark as some
wrong promise of fidelity, but to go in
as one can, empty or worshipping.
White, as a proposition. Not leprous
by easy association nor painfully radiant.
Or maybe that, yes, maybe painfully.
To go into that. As: I am walking in the city
and there is the whiteness of the houses,
little cubes of it bleaching in the sunlight,
luminous with attritions of light, the failure
of matter in the steadiness of light,
a purification, not burning away,
nothing so violent, something clearer
that stings and stings and is then
past pain or this slow levitation of joy.
And to emerge, where the juniper
is simply juniper and there is the smell
of new shingle, a power saw outside
and inside a woman in the bath,
a scent of lemon and a drift of song,
a heartfelt imitation of Bessie Smith.
The given, as in given up
or given out, as in testimony.

Faint Music

Maybe you need to write a poem about grace.

When everything broken is broken,
and everything dead is dead,
and the hero has looked into the mirror with complete contempt,
and the heroine has studied her face and its defects
remorselessly, and the pain they thought might,
as a token of their earnestness, release them from themselves
has lost its novelty and not released them,
and they have begun to think, kindly and distantly,
watching the others go about their days—
likes and dislikes, reasons, habits, fears—
that self-love is the one weedy stalk
of every human blossoming, and understood,
therefore why they had been, all their lives,
in such a fury to defend it, and that no one—
except some almost inconceivable saint in his pool
of poverty and silence—can escape this violent, automatic
life's companion ever, maybe then, ordinary light,
faint music under things, a hovering like grace appears.

As in the story a friend told once about the time
he tried to kill himself. His girl had left him.
Bees in the heart, then scorpions, maggots, and then ash.
He climbed onto the jumping girder of the bridge,
the bay side, a blue, lucid afternoon.
And in the salt air he thought about the word "seafood,"
that there was something faintly ridiculous about it.
No one said "landfood." He thought it was degrading to the rainbow perch
he'd reeled in gleaming from the cliffs, the black rockbass,
scales like polished carbon, in beds of kelp
along the coast—and he realized that the reason for the word
was crabs, or mussels, clams. Otherwise
the restaurants could just put "fish" up on their signs,
and when he woke—he'd slept for hours, curled up
on the girder like a child—the sun was going down
and he felt a little better, and afraid. He put on the jacket

he'd used for a pillow, climbed over the railing
carefully, and drove home to an empty house.

There was a pair of her lemon yellow panties
hanging on a doorknob. He studied them. Much-washed.
A faint russet in the crotch that made him sick
with rage and grief. He knew more or less
where she was. A flat somewhere on Russian Hill.
They'd have just finished making love. She'd have tears
in her eyes and touch his jawbone gratefully. "God,"
she'd say, "you are so good for me." Winking lights,
a foggy view downhill toward the harbor and the bay.
"You're sad," he'd say. "Yes." "Thinking about Nick?"
"Yes," she'd say and cry. "I tried so hard," sobbing now,
"I really tried so hard." And then he'd hold her for a while—
Guatemalan weavings from his fieldwork on the wall—
and then they'd fuck again, and she would cry some more,
and go to sleep.
                        And he, he would play that scene
once only, once and a half, and tell himself
that he was going to carry it for a very long time
and that there was nothing he could do
but carry it. He went out onto the porch, and listened
to the forest in the summer dark, madrone bark
cracking and curling as the cold came up.

It's not the story though, not the friend
leaning toward you, saying "And then I realized—,"
which is the part of stories one never quite believes.
I had the idea that the world's so full of pain
it must sometimes make a kind of singing.
And that the sequence helps, as much as order helps—
First an ego, and then pain, and then the singing.

Then Time

In winter, in a small room, a man and a woman
Have been making love for hours. Exhausted,
Very busy wringing out each other's bodies,
They look at one another suddenly and laugh.
"What is this?" he says. "I can't get enough of you,"
She says, a woman who thinks of herself as not given
To cliché. She runs her fingers across his chest,
Tentative touches, as if she were testing her wonder.
He says, "Me too." And she, beginning to be herself
Again, "You mean you can't get enough of you either?"
"I mean," he takes her arms in his hands and shakes them,
"Where does this come from?" She cocks her head
And looks into his face. "Do you really want to know?"
"Yes," he says. "Self-hatred," she says, "longing for God."
Kisses him again. "It's not what it is," a wry shrug,
"It's where it comes from." Kisses his bruised mouth
A second time, a third. Years later, in another city,
They're having dinner in a quiet restaurant near a park.
Fall. Earlier that day, hard rain: leaves, brass-colored
And smoky crimson, flying everywhere. Twenty years older,
She is very beautiful. An astringent person. She'd become,
She said, an obsessive gardener, her daughters grown.
He's trying not to be overwhelmed by love or pity
Because he sees she has no hands. He thinks
She must have given them away. He imagines,
Very clearly, how she wakes some mornings
(He has a vivid memory of her younger self, stirred
From sleep, flushed, just opening her eyes)
To momentary horror because she can't remember
What she did with them, why they were gone,
And then remembers, and calms herself, so that the day
Takes on its customary sequence once again.
She asks him if he thinks about her. "Occasionally,"
He says, smiling. "And you?" "Not much," she says,
"I think it's because we never existed inside time."
He studies her long fingers, a pianist's hands,
Or a gardener's, strong, much-used, as she fiddles

With her wineglass and he understands, vaguely,
That it must be his hands that are gone. Then
He's describing a meeting that he'd sat in all day,
Chaired by someone they'd felt, many years before,
Mutually superior to. "You know the expression
'A perfect fool,'" she'd said, and he had liked her tone
Of voice so much. She begins a story of the company
In Maine she orders bulbs from, begun by a Polish refugee
Married to a French-Canadian separatist from Quebec.
It's a story with many surprising turns and a rare
Chocolate-black lily at the end. He's listening,
Studying her face, still turning over her remark.
He decides that she thinks more symbolically
Than he does and that it seemed to have saved her,
For all her fatalism, from certain kinds of pain.
She finds herself thinking what a literal man he is,
Notices, as if she were recalling it, his pleasure
In the menu, and the cooking, and the architecture of the room.
It moves her—in the way that earnest limitation
Can be moving, and she is moved by her attraction to him.
Also by what he was to her. She sees her own avidity
To live then, or not to not have lived might be more accurate,
From a distance, the way a driver might see from the road
A startled deer running across an open field in the rain.
Wild thing. Here and gone. Death made it poignant, or,
If not death exactly, which she'd come to think of
As creatures seething in a compost heap, then time.

That Music

The creek's silver in the sun of almost August,
And bright dry air, and last runnels of snowmelt,
Percolating through the roots of mountain grasses
Vinegar weed, golden smoke, or meadow rust,

Do they confer, do the lovers' bodies
in the summer dusk, his breath, her sleeping face,
Confer—, does the slow breeze in the pines?
If you were the interpreter, if that were your task.

A Story about the Body

The young composer, working that summer at an artist's colony,
had watched her for a week. She was Japanese, a painter, almost
sixty, and he thought he was in love with her. He loved her
work, and her work was like the way she moved her body, used
her hands, looked at him directly when she made amused and
considered answers to his questions. One night, walking back
from a concert, they came to her door and she turned to him and
said, "I think you would like to have me. I would like that too,
but I must tell you that I have had a double mastectomy," and
when he didn't understand, "I've lost both my breasts." The radi-
ance that he had carried around in his belly and chest cavity—like
music—withered very quickly, and he made himself look at her
when he said, "I'm sorry. I don't think I could." He walked back
to his own cabin through the pines, and in the morning he found
a small blue bowl on the porch outside his door. It looked to be
full of rose petals, but he found when he picked it up that the rose
petals were on top; the rest of the bowl—she must have swept
them from the corners of her studio—was full of dead bees.

Spring Drawing

A man thinks *lilacs against white houses,* having seen them in the farm country south of Tacoma in April, and can't find his way to a sentence, a brushstroke carrying the energy of *brush* and *stroke*

—as if he were stranded on the aureole of the memory of a woman's breast,

and she, after the drive from the airport and a chat with her mother and a shower, which is ritual cleansing and a passage through water to mark transition,

had walked up the mountain on a summer evening.

Away from, not toward. As if the garden roses were a little hobby of the dead. As if the deer pellets in the pale grass and the wavering moon and the rondure—as they used to say, upping the ante—of heaven

were admirable completely, but only as common nouns of a plainer intention, *moon, shit, sky,*

as if spirit attended to plainness only, the more complicated forms exhausting it, tossed-off grapestems becoming crystal chandeliers,

as if radiance were the meaning of meaning, and justice responsible to daydream not only for the strict beauty of denial,

but as a felt need to reinvent the inner form of wishing.

Only the force of the brushstroke keeps the lilacs from pathos— the hes and shes of the comedy may or may not get together, but if they are to get at all,

then the interval created by *if,* to which mind and breath attend, nervous as the grazing animals the first brushes painted,

has become habitable space, lived in beyond wishing.

Late Spring

And then in mid-May the first morning of steady heat,

the morning, Leif says, when you wake up, put on shorts, and that's it for the day,

when you pour coffee and walk outside, blinking in the sun.

Strawberries have appeared in the markets, and peaches will soon;

squid is so cheap in the fishstores you begin to consult Japanese and Italian cookbooks for the various and ingenious ways of preparing *ika* and *calamari*;

and because the light will enlarge your days, your dreams at night will be as strange as the jars of octopus you saw once in a fisherman's boat under the summer moon;

and after swimming, white wine; and the sharing of stories before dinner is prolonged because the relations of the children in the neighborhood have acquired village intensity and the stories take longer telling;

and there are the nights when the fog rolls in that nobody likes— hey, fog, the Miwok sang, who lived here first, you better go home, pelican is beating your wife—

and after dark in the first cool hour, your children sleep so heavily in their beds exhausted from play, it is a pleasure to watch them,

Leif does not move a muscle as he lies there; no, wait; it is Luke who lies there in his eight-year-old body,

Leif is taller than you are and he isn't home; when he is, his feet will extend past the end of the mattress, and Kristin is at the corner in the dark, talking to neighborhood boys;

things change; there is no need for this dream-compelled narration; the rhythm will keep me awake, changing.

Robert Hass

Rusia en 1931

The archbishop of San Salvador is dead, murdered by no one knows who. The left says the right, the right says provocateurs.

But the families in the barrios sleep with their children beside them and a pitchfork, or a rifle if they have one.

And posterity is grubbing in the footnotes to find out who the bishop is,

or waiting for the poet to get back to his business. Well, there's this:

her breasts are the color of brown stones in moonlight, and paler in moonlight.

And that should hold them for a while. The bishop is dead. Poetry proposes no solutions: it says justice is the well water of the city of Novgorod, black and sweet.

César Vallejo died on a Thursday. It might have been malaria, no one is sure; it burned through the small town of Santiago de Chuco in an Andean valley in his childhood; it may very well have flared in his veins in Paris on a rainy day;

and nine months later Osip Mandelstam was last seen feeding off the garbage heap of a transit camp near Vladivostok.

They might have met in Leningrad in 1931, on a corner; two men about forty; they could have compared gray hair at the temples, or compared reviews of *Trilce* and *Tristia* in 1922.

What French they would have spoken! And what the one thought would save Spain killed the other.

"I am no wolf by blood," Mandelstam wrote that year. "Only an equal could break me."

And Vallejo: "Think of the unemployed. Think of the forty million families of the hungry..."

Spring Drawing 2

A man says *lilacs against white houses, two sparrows, one streaked, in a thinning birch,* and can't find his way to a sentence.

In order to he respectable, Thorstein Veblen said, desperate in Palo Alto, a thing must be wasteful, i.e., "a selective adaptation of forms to the end of conspicuous waste."

So we try to throw nothing away, as Keith, making dinner for us as his grandmother had done in Jamaica, left nothing; the kitchen was as clean at the end as when he started; even the shrimp shells and carrot fronds were part of the process,

and he said, when we tried to admire him, "Listen, I should send you into the chickenyard to look for a rusty nail to add to the soup for iron."

The first temptation of Sakyamuni was desire, but he saw that it led to fulfillment and then to desire, so that one was easy.

Because I have pruned it badly in successive years, the climbing rose has sent out, among the pale pink floribunda, a few wild white roses from the rootstalk.

Suppose, before they said *silver* or *moonlight* or *wet grass*, each poet had to agree to be responsible for the innocence of all the suffering on earth,

because they learned in arithmetic, during the long school days, that if there was anything left over,

you had to carry it. The wild rose looks weightless, the floribunda are heavy with the richness and sadness of Europe

as they imitate the dying, petal by petal, of the people who bred them.

You hear pain singing in the nerves of things; it is not a song.

The gazelle's head turned; three jackals are eating his entrails and he is watching.

Time and Materials

Gerhard Richter: Abstrakte Bilden

1

To make layers,
As if they were a steadiness of days:

It snowed; I did errands at a desk;
A white flurry out the window thickening; my tongue
Tasted of the glue on envelopes.

On this day sunlight on red brick, bare trees,
Nothing stirring in the icy air.

On this day a blur of color moving at the gym
Where the heat from bodies
Meets the watery, cold surface of the glass.

Made love, made curry, talked on the phone
To friends, the one whose brother died
Was crying and thinking alternately,
Like someone falling down and getting up
And running and falling and getting up.

2

The object of this poem is not to annihila

To not annih

The object of this poem is to report a theft,
    In progress, of everything
That is not these words
    And their disposition on the page.

The object o   f this poem is to report a theft,
   In progre   ss of everything that exists
That is not th   ese words
   And their d   isposition on the page.

The object   of   his poe   is t   epro a theft
   In   rogres   f ever   hing   at   xists
Th   is no   ese   w rds
   And their disp sit on o   the pag

3

To score, to scar, to smear, to streak,
To smudge, to blur, to gouge, to scrape.

"Action painting," i.e.,
The painter gets to behave like time.

4

The typo would be "paining."

(To abrade.)

5

Or to render time and stand outside
The horizontal rush of it, for a moment
To have the sensation of standing outside
The greenish rush of it.

6

Some vertical gesture then, the way that anger
Or desire can rip a life apart,

Some wound of color.

The Seventh Night

It was the seventh night and he walked out to look at stars.
Chill in the air sharp, not of summer, and he wondered
if the geese on the lake felt it and grew restless
and if that was why, in the late afternoon, they had gathered
at the bay's mouth and flown abruptly back and forth,
back and forth on the easy, swift veering of their wings.
It was high summer and he was thinking of autumn,
under a shadowy tall pine, and of geese overhead on cold mornings
and high clouds drifting. He regarded the stars in the cold dark.
They were a long way off, and he decided, watching them blink,
that compared to the distance between him and them,
the outside-looking-in feeling was dancing cheek-to-cheek.
And noticed then that she was there, a shadow between parked cars,
looking out across the valley where the half-moon poured thin light
down the pine ridge. She started when he approached her,
and then recognized him, and smiled, and said, "Hi, night light."
And he said, "Hi, dreamer." And she said, "Hi, moonshine,"
and he said, "Hi, mortal splendor." And she said, "That's good."
She thought for awhile. Scent of sage or yerba buena
and the singing in the house. She took a new tack and said,
"My father is a sad chair and I am the blind thumb's yearning."
He said, 'Who threw the jade swan in the chicken soup?"
Some of the others were coming out of the house, saying goodbye,
hugging each other. She said, "The lion of grief paws
what meat she is given." Cars starting up, one of the stagehands
struggling to uproot the pine. He said, "Rifling the purse
of possible regrets." She said, "Staggering tarts, a narcoleptic moon."
Most of the others were gone. A few gathered to listen.
The stagehands were lugging off the understory plants.
Two others were rolling up the mountain. It was clear that,
though polite, they were impatient. He said, "Goodbye, last thing."
She said, "So long, apocalypse." Someone else said, "Time,"
but she said, "The last boat left Xania in late afternoon."
He said, "Goodbye, Moscow, nights like sable,
mornings like the word *persimmon*." She said,
"Day's mailman drinks from a black well of reheated coffee
in a cafe called Mom's on the outskirts of Durango." He said,

"That's good." And one of the stagehands stubbed
his cigarette and said, "OK, would the last of you folks to leave,
if you can remember it, just put out the stars?" which they did,
and the white light everywhere in that silence was white paper.

AFTERWORD

I found myself, making this selection of my poems, gravitating to work I'd done in the late seventies and early eighties, partly because it included a year spent in England and partly because it included some experiments in short prose. The themes seem to have been, mostly, men and women, and domestic life, and sexual desire, and the work of imagination. Here, as a note on poetics, is some prose written at about the same time (and condensed here).

A Note on Metonymy

Just down from the mountains, early August. Lugging my youngest child from the car, I notice that his perfectly relaxed body is getting heavier every year. When I undress his slack limbs, he wakes up enough to mumble, "I like my own bed," then falls back down, all the way down, into sleep. The sensation of his weight is still in my arms as I shut the door.

In our bed, in a bundled parti-colored mass of grandmother's quilt, our eldest son. Aspirin on the dresser beside the bed, Kleenex, Nicolaides's *The Natural Way to Draw*, Kerouac's *The Dharma Bums*. Twenty years old, home from the university, working construction, in love, he gets a summer cold and in our absence climbs into our bed to nurse himself.

The kitchen, with that mix of familiarity and strangeness absence gives a room, is clean and smells strongly of bruised apples still simmering from the afternoon heat. On the table a note in the large open hand of my daughter. "Sweethearts! I've gone to work. Muffins in the drawer, coffee in the fridge. Pick me up at 4."

She graduated from high school in June. Evidently she had had friends over, got up earlier than they to go to her summer job at a merry-go-round in the park. In the cleanliness of the kitchen, the large freedom of her hand, even the choice of a red pen, are written a kind of independence and command, a new delicious pleasure in herself. High school seniors, a friend remarked, are older than university freshman.

The moon is just rising at midnight. It is past half, a swollen egg, and floods the room with light. I walk around checking. Everything seems alright. Outside on the deck where they have been spread, beach towels in the moonlight.

"*If the Spectator,*" Blake wrote, "*could enter into these Images in his Imagination, approaching them on the Fiery Chariot of his Contemplative Thought... or could make a Friend & Companion of one of these Images of wonder... then would he arise from his grave, then would he meet the Lord in the Air & then would he be happy.*"

And Eliot: "*I am moved by fancies that are curled/ Around these images and cling—*"

Last summer I had written about beach towels drying on a fence at the end of August in the early morning heat. I think it pleased me as much as anything I'd written that year, but I knew that it seemed slight to everyone who saw it. I had somehow not gotten it right. If this were the seventeenth century, Japan, if I were Kikaku or Rensetsu, I would have gone to the master, Bashō, and said, "How about this? 'Beach towels drying in the moonlight.' And Bashō would have said, "Hass, you have Edo-taste. You have the weakness of trying to say something unusual. 'Beach towels drying on a fence' is perhaps not good enough. 'Beach towels drying in the moonlight' is bad, even if it seems better at first, like one of those trees that flowers but bears no fruit." Ten years or more they spent together, trying to understand how to make an image.

In our room, our son having been dislodged tactfully from the bed and sympathized with and re-settled, my wife in the lamp-light is rubbing lotion into her skin and examining mosquito bites. That morning we had been lying on warm granite beside a lake the melting snow fed and her breasts are a little sunburned.

Chekhov recorded this in his notebook: "They were mineral water bottles with preserved cherries in them." The context lost—is a mineral water bottle equivalent to a Coke bottle? What sort of diligence, refinement, husbandry do the preserved cherries imply? What summer idyl or thrift?—it still gives a small, intense thrill of pleasure. Perhaps the very lost context, like the lost context of the animals drawn on the walls of the Lascaux caves, intensifies it. What we see is not, maybe, the heart of reality toward which the image leaps, for which the mimetic impulse harbors its longing, but the quiet attention that is the form of the impulse to leap.

Because images haunt us. There is a whole mythology based on this fact. Cezanne painting till his eyes bled. Wordsworth wandering the Lake Country in an impassioned daze. Blake describes it very well and so did the colleague of Du Fu who said, "It is like being alive twice." Images are not quite ideas, they are stiller than that, with less implication outside themselves. And they are not myth, they do not have that explanatory power; they are nearer to pure story. Nor are they metaphors. They do not say this is like that, they say this is. In the nineteenth century one would have said that what compelled us about them was the sense of the eternal. And it is something like that, some feeling in the arrest of the image that what perishes and what lasts forever have been brought into conjunction, and accompanying that sensation is a feeling of release from the self. "*Hoy es siempre todavía,*" Antonio Machado wrote. Yet today is always. And Czesław Miłosz: "*Tylko trwa wieczna chwila.*" Only the moment is eternal.

For me, at least, there is a delicate balance in this matter. Because the stillness of the instant exists by virtue of its velocity. If it is eternal, it is eternal because it is gone in a second. This was the paradox Wallace Stevens must have had in mind when he wrote:

> Beauty is momentary in the mind,
>
> the fitful tracing of a portal,
> but in the flesh it is immortal.

It's this crossing of paths that the image seems to reconcile. *Seems* to reconcile, and so it haunts us.

Robert Hass
from *Twentieth Century Pleasures*
(New York: Ecco Press/HarperCollins, 1984)

Five American Poets

JOHN MATTHIAS

Born on 5 September 1941 in Columbus, Ohio, John Matthias studied literature at Ohio State University, Stanford University, and the University of London. He has also been Visiting Fellow in Poetry, and is now Life Member, at Clare Hall, Cambridge. From 1967 until his retirement he taught at the University of Notre Dame. He continues to serve as poetry editor of *Notre Dame Review*. Along with his own poetry, he has published translations, criticism, and works of scholarship. His own work has been translated into Swedish, Dutch, French, German, Greek, Italian, and Serbian. He has been the recipient of grants from the Fulbright, Lilly and Merrill Foundations.

Post-Anecdotal

I

And then what? Then I thought of
What I first remembered:
Underneath some porch with Gide.
Oh, not with Gide. But after years & years
I read that he remembered what he first
Remembered, and it was that.

II

Not this: Someone calling me,
Johnny, Johnny. I was angry, hid.
It was humid, summer, evening.
I hid there sweating in the bushes
As the dark came down. I could
Smell the D.D.T. they'd sprayed
That afternoon—it hung there in
The air. But so did the mosquitoes
That it hadn't killed. *Johnny!*
Oh, I'd not go back at all. I'd
Slammed the door on everyone

After Years Away

I My Bed, My Father's Bell

First my bed, then his, now mine again—
Just for a week.

He died in it, my father, where for years
I'd lie beside my pretty love,

Alive and indiscreet.
He moved in here so she, my mother,

Might sleep undisturbed while he gazed darkly
All night long into the dark.

In need, he'd ring a small brass bell
Molded in the shape

Of a hoop-skirted lady
Sweeping with a broom and looking grim.

I see it now,
Lying sideways on a row of books.

He'd ring it and she'd come to him.

II   My Father's Bell, My Grandfather's Books

The books are remnants of a city gardener's
Life: the works of Emerson,

A Tennyson collected, *Paradise Lost.*
He's written in his Milton

1650
<u>1608</u>

   42 years. And on the title page:
Begun in January, 1893, and never finished.

In another hand: *Happy New Year to you, 1892.*
He's figured that J.M. was 42 in 1650

When he wrote his answer to Salmasius
And lost his sight.

Defensio pro Populo Anglicano.
At the Presbyterian funeral a cousin

Asked: *are you religious?* And I said
In callow family disaffection:

Gnostic. Bogomil. Albigensian for heaven's sake.
On the *Ex Libris* plate:

Poetry. This book will not be loaned.
And underneath: *couldn't dig this month.*

Ground as cold as hell.
I replace the book, I pick up the bell.

III   My Mother's Broom, My Father's Bell

My mother stashed those books in here
For me to find. My father

Would have seen them, reaching for hs bell,
But they were not for him.

She left them here, her father's only legacy,
As she began to sweep.

She swept the hearth, the porch and drive,
She even swept the street.

(She swept my father once entirely
off his feet.)

While he lay dying & while I sat reading books,
She swept his mortal breath away,

I think.
When she heard the ringing here

And then swept circles round & round the bier
And I said *Gnostic, Bogomil.*

Although the ground was cold as hell
They dug the grave & dug it deep.

John Matthias

Sweet sleep. Sweep sweep.
There's no one here to listen or to care,

And so I ring the bell—
Creating great commotion *there.*

Rhododendron

Several years ago, you planted
Near my study window something green.
Today I notice it, not just green,

But blazing red-in-green exactly
Like the rhododendron it turned out
To be when you said: *Look!*

My rhododendron's flowering.
As usual, I had never asked, had
Never noticed, would not have

Had an answer if our daughter or
Her friend had said a day ago: *And that?*
Just what is that? It's something green,

I'd have had to say, *that your mother*
Planted there, some kind of flower
That hasn't flowered yet, although

She planted it three years ago.
It's the word itself, I think, that's
Made it flower, and your saying it.

The winter's not been easy, and the
Spring's been slow. I stared at long white
Papers full of emptiness and loss

As one might stare at rows of narrow
Gardens full of snow. The words
Have not come easily, have not come well.

Easily you tell me, stepping through
The door: *Look! My rhododendron's
Flowering…* And it is, and it does.

Everything To Be Endured

for Ernest Sandeen

   …everything to be endured
You said, quoting Matthew Arnold,
And nothing to be done.
No fit theme for poetry. And I
Remembered, sometime or other in school,
Reading that. About *Empedocles*
On Etna—and then, I think, in Yeats,
Who quoted it excluding Wilfred Owen from
His *Oxford Book of Modern Verse.*
You looked at me, hoping I would
Understand, and yet I hadn't… Because
You meant your own poems, those
You write and show to no one, those
That lie down darkly in some bottom drawer—
Those, you thought, that did no more
Than imitate a passive suffering.
I should have known.

But then what's passive
When a man of eighty-five, survivor
Of two cancers, sits up all night long
To face his demons in the way he always has
And sees at dawn the black rectangle
On his desk he's made of darkness
Hurled at eternity in words?
This is something to be done,
Endured to be everything, fit theme

For any poem. Poems in the mind,
Poems in the bottom drawer,
Poems heading out past Jupiter like
Mental probes launched at some far sun.
They're all the same.

You wouldn't choose
To write these poems but you are chosen.
That's endurance and the doing
And the fitness all in one. Where they go
And what becomes of them you'll never know.
If you kneel down before the winter hearth
To burn them, who's to say they'll not
Be etched by fire on some unheard of stone
Standing somewhere in an unknown city?

Not Having Read

for William, Teresa, and Joe

Not having read a single fairy tale
For a long long time
Because my children now are grown,
I buy a book of them for the child of friends
And later get caught up in it alone
Waiting nervously beside the phone
For word of an adult.

Once there was a cat
Who made acquaintance of a rat.
There was a peasant once
Who drove his oxen with a heavy load of wood.
An ugly fisherman lived with an ugly wife
In an ugly shack beside the heaving sea.
A man was rich, another man was poor.
A father called his children in before him.
Once there was a little girl
Whose mother and father had died.
Once there was a witch.

Time passes. It is late.
Outdoors the wind is howling, and it rains.
My beard turns gray and
Grows between my legs, grows
Across the carpet, down the basement stairs.
The house creaks. The globe
Spins off its axis, smashes on the floor.

The telephone is ringing off the hook.
My daughter is all right.

Francophiles, 1958

La transhumance du Verbe, incanted René Char.
And so we would repasture
in the tower-room and try to think in French
directed by a *berger* from Morocco. Frogs were in.
Brits and Yanks were out. Hell was other people
we'd proclaim, pointing out each other's *mauvaise foi*.
What was not absurd was certainly surreal, essence rushing
headlong at existence all the way from Paris to
Vaucluse. Over hills we sent our sheep with Cathar heretics—
through unsettled valleys into settled code. (One day
predatory age would eat our lambs, but that was
too far off to see): We went to bed with both Bardot
and de Beauvoir. Fantastic volunteers of *Le Maquis*, we
knew about Algeria, about
Dien Bien Phu...
                                    Camus was in,
Steinbeck clearly out.
Sartre had overestimated novels by Dos Pasos.
Pesos paid the wage of Sisyphus to roll
his boulder up the hill;
dollars went a good long way on continental holidays
if you could catch the Maître's mistress
mouthing his enciphered wholly unacknowledged
fully legislative & heraldic letter: *d'*...

But S.O.E. and F.L.N. were not on anybody's SATs.
No trees blossomed into Hypnos Leaves.
No one gave us arms.
No one's army occupied our town, and not
a single paratrooper dangled in his harness from our tower.
Camus declared in Stockholm: *I'm no existentialist.*
But if obliged to choose between the works
of Justice and ma mère, I will choose ma mère.
That surprised us as we greedily
claimed Justice for our own—which was easy
with our mothers safe at home & cooking us authentic dinners
that we ate like old conspirators in jails.

Still, the poet transcribed secret words
directly in his poems.
They named the roads, the villages, coordinates for
sabotage, assassination, unforeseen attacks.
We heard a beeping in the wires, the bleating
of a little flock, a change of key in those reiterations
by Ravel when music, like the Word,
tumbles starving into green transhumant fields.

Smultronstället

    … and someone saying, *Yes*
but Göran doesn't really speak good Swedish.
I looked up, perplexed.
Skanian, he declared. *He's from the south,*
as all of us—Doctor Isak Borg and Marianne,
Sarah, Anders, and Viktor;
Susan, John and G. Printz-Påhlson—
headed down to Malmö and to Lund.
Smultron's not the same as jordgubbe said
a man in dark glasses sitting right behind us in
the Lane Arts Cinema, Columbus, 1959:
a handless clock, a coffin falling from the hearse,
and top-hatted ancients walking to their

jubeldoktor honors, Borg having dreamed
his way from Stockholm, Sarah both his lost love
and late Fifties girl, just like my Susan, flirting
with the guys in the back seat, chewing on her pipe.
What did I know then of time, of memory, of age?
And who would watch a movie wearing heavy shades?
We looked behind us and he nodded in a formal way.
Göran, ten years my senior, was writing poems
in Malmö that von Sydow liked to read—*Max*,
as he called him, who spoke his Swedish very well
whether as a knight in *The Seventh Seal*
or there before us pumping gas in *Smultronstället*
or when reading Göran's poems to a little
group of connoisseurs. But Max doesn't
get it when the doctor says, mostly to himself,
Perhaps I should have stayed.
We didn't get it either, though we stayed—right
through the film, and trying very hard.
In twenty years I'd introduce my friend from Skania
to my Midwest as Dr. Printz-Påhlson, poet.
A colleague thought that Göran was a royal and
called him *Prince*. Oh, and Göran hated
Bergman films, all that religious angst, which
everybody asked about, even though his lecture was
on Strindberg. So much for the 80s.
In 1959 Bibi Anderson was twenty-two, only
three years older than my girlfriend.
I thought how much I'd like to sleep with her.
The man in sun glasses put his head between us
and said, <u>*Place*</u> *of wild strawberries;*
the English doesn't get it. The car drove on.
Years after Göran got his own degree at Lund, his head
literally belaurelled, little girls in white
throwing flower petals in his path,
he fell all humpty-dumpty down a flight of stairs
and broke his crown on the concrete, and lost
his sight, and pushed aside his work, and rests
in silence in a Malmö nursing home. With whom
share a joke, a plate of herrings, bog myrtle schnapps?
The nightmare examiner had said:

You are guilty of guilt
when Isak Borg mis-diagnosed his patient, saying
She is dead. You are incompetent, concluded the
examiner, and all of us got back into the car
and headed south: Borg & Marianne; Sarah, Anders, Victor;
Susan, John, & Goran; and the man in heavy shades.
The summer sun is blinding, even in the night.
Smultronstället. Wherever we were from,
we couldn't stay.

My Mother's Webster

She'd never tell me how to spell a word;
Go look it up, she'd say. She'd say *It's there in Webster,*
pointing to the battered blue and dog-eared dictionary
that she'd lugged from Georgetown to Columbus long
before those Anglo-Saxon expletives she said offended her
entered the American Heritage. I find it at the bottom of a box
unpacking things I thought to save when she turned vague,

lost the words she'd loved, and started groping for a few
remembered monosyllables to get her through a day of
meals, treatments, therapies, and baths at Olentangy Home.
Her house is sold; she's 92; and I decide to look it up
when I'm unsure about how one spells *Houyhnhnm*
and want to write a footnote citing Swift in *Gulliver.*
The facing page is black with marginalia; it's in her hand.

What alchemy is this? *A curse on Sally Smothers*
she has written, circled, arrowed to *hostility*
in one direction, *hothead* in another. *Turn the page*
she writes, and there beside the underlined *horned toad*
and *hornet* she abbreviates, S.S., with arrows to *horrendous.*
She writes: *My friends: Eleanor, Elizabeth, and Jean.*
She writes: *The boy I do not love: Jason Dean: ZZ.*

Some words are simply canceled: *housewife* with an X,
hooker with a line; the illustrations under *horseshoe*
toss her up to *horah*, ring her to *hosanna*; *horn of plenty* is
a *cornucopia*, and that is circled six or seven times.
Next to *horologe* she writes *ding-ding* and clearly likes
hornswoggle, prints in little caps: *They'll do it every time.*
She writes *I'll host a hostage in the hostel, my hors d'oeuvre!*

Who is this language sprite? It seems to be my mother
talking to herself in 1917. There's still heavy fighting on
the Western Front; her father has just died; she'll meet *my* father
in another seven years. There is no sulfa yet, no penicillin;
Eleanor and Jean will get the post-war flu and not survive.
I've never heard her mention Jason Dean. She will, in fact,
become a housewife and she'll outlive Sally Smothers

that old hothead she called *hornet* and *horned toad*.
The goddesses of seasons, Horae, might have taught her
in good time a ripe Horatian patience as she gazed
at *horoscope* and then *horizon*—looked up from the page
and out her bedroom window at the *horos*, boundary,
tangent plane across the surface of the globe defining
the conjunction of the earth and sky. She writes:

I guess that means about as far as I can see.
There's not a mark here or an indication that she saw her
future linked to *hospital* or *hospice*—
nor to *Houyhnhnms*, rational and gentle creatures
one might like for neighbors even at the Olentangy Home
and whose name I cannot spell. I can hear her say again
Well go and look it up, it's there in Webster,

meaning this particular blue book, and not some other.
I'd look her up herself if I could find her. She's always in,
but she is never there. She's here in 1917 and not hornswoggled
or intimidated or a hostage in some hostel where they
do it every time. There's a horseshoe on her door.
There's not a single cloud on the horizon and it's June.
She'll be her own hors d'oeuvre and dance the horah round

a horn of plenty. She writes: *I'm Thirteen in Three Days.*

Diminished Third

I Expectation

The woman clad in white, large red roses
shedding petals from her dress, expects
the unexpected, wanders through a moonlit wood
where, God knows, anyone might stumble
on their lover's corpse...
                                        Even Schoenberg
in Vienna in *Erwartung*, improvising
ostinatos, overriding bars, or Hohenzollern Isoldes
spiking Bismark helmets at the stars—

Even Moses, who could only speak, exclaiming
Ich will singen,
counting on his finger tips the laws.

II Doctor Faust

Boxed by Thomas Mann into a magic square
with megrims, paedophiles and fictive sounds,
A.S. rages over stolen property, the rape and insult
perpetrated by this syphilitic Leverkühn who writes

a serialism no one ever heard. And yet he'd said himself
that music was a word, that language was a kind
of music too: Had in fact some rowdy losal out of hell
so pricked his blood with sophistries that nosey

novelists could smell the sulphur in his permutations?
Did *Volk* and *Führer* grow dodecaphonic in his
retrogrades, inversions; Hetaera Esmaralda somehow

ciphered in the h-e-a-e flat of it? *Sator Arepo
tenet opera rotas.* The opera would circle, right enough.
And the sower would sue for his tenet. In tenebrae.

III   The Golden Calf

Aron, was hast du getan

This sprechstimme! This old dogmatic honky rapper
here before his time among the Angels.
He'd lecture all the Jews as all the Jews go down
all over Europe. He's safe and sound. His friend
is Mr. Gershwin and he beats the younger man
at tennis, ping pong, chess. He cannot win a Guggenheim,
cannot get performed.

Around him nothing but the idols
and the kitsch and the clichés. He's heard that in this
land of plenty no one gets a second act;
he cannot score a third and that's a fact.
Still the old Dodecaphon speaks while Aaron sings:
Ich will singen dinga dinga ding!
Anyone might stumble on a lover's corpse.

Is he Moses, Aaron, or their contradiction burning
in his brain like Leverkühn's disease?
Darf das Leid, mein Mund, dieses Bild machen?
Gershwin whistles happily: *I got plenty o' nuttin.*
Schoenberg spricht like eine glückliche hand:
Das Grenzenlose! Boundlessness!
Constellation upon constellation whirls.
Harmonielehre multiplies
by twelves through some 2000 bars and dies
with Volk and Fürher.
So if the end, as Schnabel says, will justify the means,
you might as well have a nice day.
Why not keep on smiling while you
take the line of most resistance, even in L.A.?

A Note on Barber's Adagio

for Dónal Gordon

...Back in autumn 1963
Samuel Barber was alone and driving through
November rain in Iowa or Kansas.
When he turned on his radio he heard
Them playing his *Adagio for Strings*.
Sick to death of his most famous composition,
He turned the dial through the static
Until once again, and clearly—
The *Adagio for Strings*. When a third station, too,
And then a fourth, were playing it, he thought
He must be going mad. He turned off the radio
And stopped the car and got out by a fence
Staring at the endless open space in front of him
Where someone on a tractor plowed
On slowly in the rain...

The president had been assassinated
Earlier that day, but Barber didn't know it yet.
He only knew that every station in America was playing
His *Adagio for Strings*.
He only knew he didn't know
Why he should be responsible for such an ecstasy of grief.

Four Seasons of Vladimir Dukelsky

I Winter

...and the Winter Palace stormed.
Place where khaki tall Kerensky
Felt the fire Scriabin fanned at everything provisional in his *Prometheus*.
He'd huff and puff and blow down what was hardly built.
Crew-cut Angel Gabriel with sex appeal, Dukelsky said of K.
Dukelsky—hot Kiev Conservatory music-man whose own angelic
Sex appeal took the form of Debussy pastiche,
Aladdine & Palomide his *Pelléas.*

Would K. play Melisande all dressed in skirt and head scarf
Fleeing commissars who paid Dukelsky in potatoes, rice and peas
For a revolutionary hymn *à la* Glazunov? Newly beggared
Vladimir, obliged to drink a tea he made from bark & carrots,
Wore an avant-garde green coat his mother cut from
Billiard-table baize, shirt and trousers that
Had been the winter curtains in his late father's room. He thought he heard
A turbine buzzing somewhere in augmented fourths.

Modus diaboli! Cheka spies all whispering in Tristan's
Tritones and diminished fifths. He missed the Maeterlinck Express
From Kiev to Odessa, clicking down the rails chromatically
From C sharp on to G to conjure fields full of fauns with double flutes.
He took the typhus train, hand & handkerchief to mouth & nose
For more than fifteen days of unrelenting plague.
He hummed the *Marseillaise: En-fants*: a fourth. *Pa-trie*, a fourth again.
His mother, *ancien régime*, hid two diamonds up her snatch.

II Spring

And they escaped. What month was it, Paris? What week in New York?
In Constantinople you could hardly tell. In Odessa they had fled
The rearing horses at the gate, the Red Cavalry, the panic, mobs.
Navaho had pushed through ice behind *St. Andrew*, snow and fog
Obscuring Bosphorus for the listing Motherland's ancient ship of refugees.
Yok, Yok, Effendi sang the foxtrotting girls; and Tommies drunk on

Turkish beer demanded *Tipperary*, *K-K-K-Katy*, from the salon trio
At Tokatlian's café. Dukelsky played for silent films most anything he chose.

It was a job. Glazunov for Westerns, Mussorgsky's "Pictures"
For the Chaplins and some Rimsky-Korsakov for Lang's *Metropolis*.
One night at the Tokatlian he heard a thing he liked. They called it *Swanee*.
The boys in the native band with gusle, oud, and zourna
Made it sound like someone's jihad on the boil, but he heard the
Gershwin somehow coming through. *Yok, Yok, Effendi, it is not beloved*
By the authorities but Yanks and Limeys ask for it and "Hindustan."
He memorized it on the spot; it finally felt like spring.

When he reached New York he played the gypsy schmaltz required
For the eateries like Samovar on Second Avenue. He scored
A hooker's favorite songs for fifty cents a piece. His secret life was
Briefly all dodecaphonic when he met the man whose *Swanee* he
Had whistled on the decks of *King Alexander* on his way to an
Ellis Island transit. *Don't fear lowbrow, Kid*, he said; *Tin Pan Alley*
Is okay. If you haven't got a melody you ain't American. Heat me up
Some ragtime. We'll change that longhair name to Vernon Duke.

III   Summer

But he was not yet American, even after he prepared his friend's
Rhapsody in Blue for two pianos. His mother sold her diamonds to
An underworld dealer and sent him off to Paris where Diaghilev
Disparaged Duke for vaudeville gigs & rags but commissioned something
Neoclassical and Russian from Dukelsky: *Tutus with Kokoshniks*,
As he said. Enter Flora, lifted high by Zephyrus, dancing *pas de deux*
In an Anacreontic light. The waltz, mazurka, variations & *divertissements*
Des muses: They would even make a corpse dance, said Prokofiev.

Dukelsky still was only twenty-two. The critics liked him. Poulenc
And Stravinsky were impressed, and he got a check for 6,000 francs
And an invitation from Diaghilev to come along to London with the show.
Cocteau, however, slapped him with a glove: *Les Parisiens t'envoyent*
De la merde! But when pressed in earnest for a choice between the swords
And pistols, he sang out: *Embrassons-nous!* Degas had said to Whistler
That he dressed as if he had no talent, Gershwin wrote to D. And D. to G.:
I wish my talent didn't sometimes wear a pretty little frilly frock.

Five American Poets

He felt a little less Dukelsky, started feeling Duke. Economies would soon
Be on the rocks, Zephyrus and Flora on the dole. Would there be a
Space to occupy between an Ogden Nash and Mandelstam? He'd set them
Both to music in the end. Certain words he'd dare to write himself:
Glittering crowds & shimmering clouds in canyons of steel. Jaded roués
And gay divorcées who lunch at the Ritz. He thought about the autumn
In New York. Why did it seem so inviting? It was 1928 and he took
Another ship. Like Mandelstam in *Epitaph*, he wrapped a rose in furs.

IV   Autumn

Diaghilev soon died, and Gershwin shortly after. Dukelsky grasped at
Balanchine, the movies. Émigré composers headed for L.A. as
Wall Street crashed and Sunset Boulevard survived. Prokofiev heckled him
From Moscow about *maids who become prostitutes to feed their mums.*
His mother ate. He wrote his songs: *April in Paris* on a tuneless upright
In the back of West Side Tony's bistro; *Words Without Music* for
The Ziegfeld Follies, 1936. Duke would dig Dukelsky from the rubble
Of Depression. Dancers kicked their can-cans on the silver screen.

But did Dukelsky dig the tunes of Duke? Count Basie would in time,
Sinatra would—and, born on his own birthday, even Thelonius Monk.
Can you play again, Sam Goldwyn asked him laughing, *that dyspeptic chord?*
Musicologists have praised the two adjacencies preceding an initial E,
The lower raised chromatically to match the half step in a symmetry:
A-pril in Par-is. Meanwhile, Mandelstam still lived, weeping for
The wooden Russia of his youth. *Gradually the servants sort out piles*
Of overcoats. They wrap a rose in furs. In Cyrillic and for choir, an epitaph.

For whom? Diaghilev? Dukelsky? Mandelstam? Academic serialism
Shut down tonal elegists and Tin Pan Alley crooners came to terms
With Elvis after yet another World War. Who remembered the bucolic
Zephyrus, phantasmagoric *Epitaph* for choir? Alexander Feodorovich
Kerensky hummed a phrase stuck in his head from something that he couldn't
Name and walked the Stanford campus in the twilight to his little office
Where he wrote a book about the Revolution no one read. He wrapped
A rose in furs & it was autumn: in Leningrad & Paris, Palo Alto & New York.

Two in New York

I   Easter 1912

His name was Frédéric Sauser his name
was Blaise Cendrars his name was Nineteen Twelve
his name was Eiffel Tower.

Only later Sonia Delauny and Trans-Siberian Prose,
later loss of a good right arm at the Marne.
His name that day it was Pâques might have been Ray—

Ray of Gourmont that Easter and everyone gone.
Nobody liturgy nobody nun nobody
anthem or song or prelate or incense or drum.

So *dict nobis quid vidisti*: nobody nobody there
when he woke and wrote down his name
in New York it was Fear. What could he do but go home?

II   Christmas 1929

And what could *he* do, Chien Andalou,
whose speech had the fire of flamenco guitar,
whose eyes were the gypsies of war.

Federico gracias gracias (loricated legionaries
looking like a Guardia Civil before its time,
the Harlem jazzmen blowing bagels from the bells

of saxophone and horn: *Christus natus est*)—
Feed the poor on *cante jondo*, give the weary rest.
But what could he do, Chien Andalou,

Poeta en Nueva York? Shiva looked like Ramadan.
And yet the girls were rain. He'd ransom every
singing boy he'd die for, and he'd die for it in Spain.

Two in Harar

I Sir Richard Burton, 1854

He learned Somali from the soft and plaintive voice
of Kadima who allowed him to remove the leather lace
stitching up her labia and put two fingers in.

This was anthropology, linguistics. Topology and trade
would come in turn. Calling himself Haji Mirza Abdullah,
he wore a silken girdle with a dirk & chewed on khat

he found sufficiently priapic that in time he'd force his
member through infibulations of the local girls
without unlacing first. Now he rose and went to work.

He'd play the Amir off against al-Haji Sharmakay
on matters touching eunuchs and the slaves.
He'd demonstrate Koranic scholarship, say *Allahu Akhbar*.

He'd mesmerize them with his tales from the *Nights*.
His exegesis of *The Sura* dazzled all the mullahs
and he wisely took a local *abban* from among the Isas.

By the southwest coast near Zayla he turned inland,
riding on a donkey with a shotgun on his knee.
Everything that was not stone was sand. Everything that

was not sun was dust and wind. His bodyguards were
Long Gulad, The Hammal, End of Time.
They sang him Belwos, fed him holcus for his colic,

millet beer and boiled barks. If the nomads took him
he would learn phallotomy, his penis gone
for scholarship among the wives in someone's tent.

Bedu lurked about his camp and hurled stones.
They called him Old Woman, Chief of Zayla, Painted Man.
They called him Turk & Priest & Pilgrim—Merchant,

Banyan, and Calamity Sent Down from God.
He gave up his disguise and forged a letter from the
Aden consul introducing him as an ambassador

and dressed up in his captain's uniform with
epaulets and sword. He marched until he saw the walls
no white man ever breached, the gate he thought

he'd walk through chanting poems. Back in Zayla
they proclaimed him dead. Back in London
Karl Marx & Tennyson sat down to read his Mecca Haj.

The Amir asked him if he'd come to buy Harar.

II   Arthur Rimbaud, 1886–1888

And was Harar for sale? And were *Le Voyant*'s visions
null and void? *Solde*. He'd left behind what time
nor science had acknowledged, drowned his book of magic

and returned to earth. And one must enter splendid cities
absolutely modern after all. Among the packs
of one-eyed mangy dogs. And with a taste for soil & stone.

His I was other and another still. His ear once made
him brass and like a bugle he had blown.
A scent of wood, he'd found himself a broken violin.

He did not think he knew and did not want to know
how he'd been thought into his poems.
He colored vowels no more and all of them went black.

He'd be a gun-butt now if he were wood;
if he were steel, a rail laid down in Africa for desert trains.
He studied business, engineering, crafts.

He'd sold unknown harmonic intervals for
proper calculation and would traffic
in the hides and coffee-beans and ivories of Somalia

living by the Raouf Pasha palace earning two percent
commission from Pierre Bardey on trade.
And when the Mahdi rose and Dervishes advanced

through Abyssinia, he mocked Khartoum's illuminated
English Gordon, rich Egyptians & the Turks,
and took a caravan of armaments on inland from Tajoura

and was ruined. He came back to Harar and tried to run
the trading station while in Paris decadents
proclaimed a system based entirely on his Sonnet of the Vowels.

Black A, white E, red I, blue O, green U.
Was he back where he belonged? This wasn't what Parnassians
had in mind. They might proclaim King Menelek

himself a symbolist if he became Negasti & Hararis were
his businessmen of Empire up and down their narrow streets.
There was no Amir left in town, no Wazir.

Sultan Ahmad bin Sultan Abibakr had asked Captain Burton
if he'd come to buy Harar. The poet advertised the sale
of priceless bodies, *hors de toute race, hors de toute monde.*

Travelers would not render their commission for a while.

She Maps Iraq

She maps Iraq. For England and for Empire
and the Man Who Would Be King.
She is Miss Gertrude Bell, a friend of T.E.L.
and Faisal. She knows much more

than all the men around her table, and she knows
they know this and despise her for her
knowledge and her fluent Arabic. They need her though,
and so she maps Iraq. They cannot find

a thing: no well or wall or wildflower blooming
where they all think nothing blooms.
What they know they only say to one another
at their club—*conceited silly flatchest windbag daughter*

of the Ironworks Bell & Bell. They'd all
sweat their smelting jealousies in Turkish baths.
She maps Iraq. They all take notes. They lean across
her table, light her endless cigarettes.

She was in love with Doughty-Wylie, Charles Doughty's
nephew who could quote in Persian poetry
that she translated back in 1893 with her lost Cadogan—
Songs of dying laughter, songs of love once warm.

Churchill sent D-Wylie to Gallipoli to die a hero and so now
she maps Iraq for Churchill, too. *And still a graver*
music runs beneath the tender love notes of
those songs she murmurs to herself, her pencil poised.

She'd loved dear old Cadogan, too, but Hugh
the foundry magnate Bell opposed a marriage with this man
of so few prospects, and she loved her brilliant father
most of all. (The gossips had her now in love with Faisal.)

At tea with Mrs. Humphrey Ward or Jenny Lind
or Henry James she used to say: *I know your work*, and
I shall go to Oxford. At Balliol, she was obliged
to sit in lectures on the history of Empire with her back

to tutor Mr. Black, and yet she got a First in spite of that,
and now she maps Iraq. There was ancient Hit
where Babylonians found oil to light their lamps. And here
was Ukhaidir, her own discovery & gift to archeology,

or so she hoped, in photographs & sketches, measurements
of every kind. They wrote down in their notes *Petroleum at Hit*
and made no reference to the ruins at Ukhaidir.
Arabia Deserta was beside her even now, whispering

archaic Englishes that Doughty drew from Spenser,
whispering his nephew's name. She'd lead a gift-mare through
the very room and not a single hand would offer her
a sheep's eye or a carpet full of pillows on the desert sand.

She maps Iraq. She thinks their nodding heads resemble camels'
and she almost laughs remembering just yesterday
when Churchill slid from his high saddle on a camel's hump
in front of Lawrence & the Sphinx. She says that Baghdad,

Bosrah, Mosul should be *vilayets* but unified by the Sharif
the French drove out of Syria—the French, whose
archeologists wrote up her finds at Ukhaidir before she
published *Amurath to Amurath*. The camels' heads nod on.

She says and here is Carchemish where all the Hittites
watched through their binoculars as Germans
built the Baghdad railway bridge. Had they visited
Assyrians in Kalat Shergat, all the Jewish tribes there in Haran?

She'd wager none of them had been detained by the Rashids
but she was in a harem at Hayil back when Ibn Saud marched
that way before the war. She wonders now how many of
those pills she took. Lawrence would be difficult for wives

of all these men, but she herself was thought to be impossible.
Doughty-Wiley had a wife, and so did Cox, and even
Faisal, although no one ever saw her. They said her own visits
to the sheiks were scandalous where she was treated

as an honorary man. She smoked with them and drank their
bitter coffee and could gallop their best horses
with their favorite sons. Here were twelve oases and
the routes to them and these were villages one shouldn't

for a moment underestimate. Faisal held her once so long
she felt she couldn't breathe, but then he only kissed her hand.
She still read Doughty-Wiley's letters in the night.
But where exactly draw these lines demarking Syria and

Palestine Iraq Arabia & Jordan Britain & the French had made
agreements while the Zionists had wondered was she Arab
or an English woman in her Bond Street skirts and funny hats.
It made her very tired. They said her influence had waned

but gave her titles both officially and otherwise: It was perhaps
too many of those pills she took to sleep.
She maps Iraq, but cannot now recall if in her wild travels
she had seen what she had said: *I know your work*, and

I shall go to Oxford. She was Oriental Secretary and she had
an O.B.E. She was Director of Antiquities in Baghdad
at her own museum. *And still a graver music runs beneath
the tender love notes of those songs* did not translate

Petroleum at all. She's feeling very thirsty now for water
and not oil, speaks to them of dizziness, a spell, some word
you don't pronounce as it is written or a place you've
never been that seems to be familiar as your English home.

The men stand up around her map and someone says
It isn't here and she says *but I've told you that was lost.*
Everybody leaves. They pluck their camels' heads
right off their shoulders as they go and she is back at Balliol

or in her bed and *Who said anything about Americans*
she'd give this land to Fattuh, her dear servant, or to Hugh,
her father, and you see there on her map Northumbria
is clearly indicated as a corner of this world.

She longs for sleep in which her map would gather her
into its folds and roll her up as in a carpet taken
from the desert floor. Daughter of a foundry, she has been
a maid of Iron. For she has mapped Iraq...

whispers only... *Faisal, Fattuh, Father, take me back.*

Persistent Elegy

*Shortly before the 1994 South African election my former student, Clare Stewart,
was murdered in KwaZulu, probably by an Inkatha hit squad.*

And now at last Nelson Mandela's elected.
But what of my student, Clare?
Would she have danced as she had expected?
They don't even number the dead in Rwanda.
She raises her hand in the air.
What did she do in KwaZulu to anger Inkatha?

She sits in my class long ago taking notes.
This is my student, Clare.
Volunteers have busily counted the votes.
She wakes to the voices of children.
Her daughter's among them there.
What did she do in KwaZulu to anger Inkatha?

No volunteers can describe what nobody sees.
She leaves a note in the mission.
She walks by the lake, the flowering trees.
Observers say the election is fair.
She gets in a pick-up, drives from the village.
She raises her hand in the air.

She tries to answer the question.
What did you do in KwaZulu to anger Inkatha?
What is the answer, Clare?
They don't even number the dead in Rwanda.
Nobody's counting there.
But what did she do in KwaZulu to anger Inkatha?

She raises her hand in the air.
And now at last Nelson Mandela's elected.
What of my student, Clare?
She never arrives where she is expected.
Everyone's weeping there.
What did she do in KwaZulu to anger Inkatha?

What of my student, what of my student, Clare?

Walter's House

Passing on the Campion, for Cornelius Eady

I know it's Walter's house no longer,
But I think of it, because I've thought of it
That way for thirty years and more,
As Davis Place. For far too long it was
Entirely empty. When I was young and just
Had come to town, he welcomed me,
Passing on *The Works of Thomas Campion*
He'd edited that very year, 1967.
It was the year I married. It was a year
When one could still persuade oneself
That the Sixties, whose veterans now are sixty,
Might in fact still usher in Aquarius by way
Of a machinery concealed by some Inigo
Within the fantasy of its extraordinary masque
Performed in Caesar's court...

   From our house to yours,
The inscription reads, *with hopes*

For every kind of harmony forever. I'd sit there
In his study imitating gruff Yvor Winters
Gruffly reading *Now Winter Nights*, and claim
That I had Stanford friends—Pinsky,
Hass and Peck—who had written poems already
That would matter. He drank too much,
Like Winters, and he told me in his cups
The price he'd paid for scholarship, the expense
Of spirit and the loss of years in dusty rooms
And half-lit archives. But his study was ablaze
With light and insight.

                              When winter nights enlarged
The number of their hours, I'd walk South Bend's
Park Avenue and wish it were New York's.
Sometimes very late, one or two a.m., I'd pass his house
And see the beam across the snow from where his
Curtains didn't meet. He was still up and working.
First at his desk, then at the harpsichord, the Gamba,
Picking out an aire, testing theory against meter against
Song—*Goe, numbers, boldly pass*—with speaking voice
And then with instruments... In 1600 there went forth
From Campion a treatise where, he said,
It was "demonstratively proved" that
Quantitative counting was not cant in English.
Walter loved the massed sounds of strophes all full
Of l's and e's and o's, or lines all keyed to single
Vowel: *O then I'le shine forth as an Angell of light.*
He played through scales in tetra chords, listened
For the semitones, and anchored counterpointing
With the bass. *Nympha potens Thamesis*
Soli cessura Dianae raised her head above the ice
Of Campion's Latin verse. The Thames
Was the St. Joseph River, and the lady listened with me
In the night. She counted quantities
But looked like Bessie Smith. We thought we heard

A new music in that house that for so long
Was still. A poet filling up the walls again with books,
The study as a student of the word & song.

Among the maskers linger ghostly Lords like Scrope & North,
But Counts like Basie, Dukes like Ellington, emerge.
The innovative chords are Monk's.
When we walk along the street at night
We think we hear the lute of Muddy Waters
And Chicago Blues...

                    Cornelius, I thought I'd
Pass on Thomas Campion because he lived so long in
Walter's mind who lived so long where you've arrived,
Bringing with you poetries to make a madrigal
Of time and circumstance, contingencies
And synchronicity. Take what you've said—*a motion,*
Gambling's pitch, holding back and laying out,
Slow-mo chop-time logic lifted up & then away that
You can sing. Invite Walt Davis to the house warming
With his book of ayres, his sackbuts and his
Gambas and his viols... And then shine forth.
Then shine forth like Angels.

O then shine forth like Angels of the light.

Tsunami: The Animals

Not very many animals died. The human beings, sucked
Out of their windows, plucked from one another's arms, may
Have heard the trumpeting of elephants, may have seen
Flamingos group and leave for inland forests, boars and
Monkeys heading for a higher ground. Do even fish that
Swim in grand aquariums of restaurants where we eat
The flesh and organs of clairvoyants on some 87th floor
Detect the tremor we don't feel until we crash through
Ceilings in a fall of rubble upside down, a fork impaled
In an eye? Are the creatures then an ark? Noah, no one knows.
Does the trunk laid flat upon the earth before a trumpeting
Begins detect an earthquake or tsunami in the human heart
As well as movement of tectonic plates, approaching footsteps

Of a man who'd rather be a bomb? A flood, a flash of
Detonation. Caged canaries in our common mine
Burst through bars in song. High in heaven's Yala,
Water buffalo are shaking off the waters of the world's woe.

Swell

I

The lake was swell that year. The fishing too
was swell both there and in the rivers, but especially swell
was that one lovely girl among the group from
Horton Bay. It was 1920 and he'd lived
somehow through shelling at Fossalta di Piave that
he'd write about, and then escaped the influenza
which had killed more people than the war itself,
among them Edward, eldest son of my own
Grandfather M., himself a veteran of the Spanish War
and Spanish flu...
                    In 1950 there I am
with my one fish, a bass. I caught it trolling from a boat
in Walloon Lake and someone took my picture
holding it up high. That's the full extent of my experience
and success as angler. But it was swell that day.
I was ten and I'd been on the lake since dawn.
They all say things are swell in early Hemingway.
We say things are great, even when they're not, even
when they're only fair-to-middling, even when
they're only average to a fault. Great time. Great lake.
Great girl. Those things that were swell.
We say it sometimes with a lean sarcastic sneer
and sometimes really mean it.

Two or three years later I began to read him.
I thought he was just great. Who didn't in those days
before they wrote his life, counted up his whiskies and his pills,
and told his secrets as he went to seed somewhere out in Idaho

and at the Mayo Clinic where they gave him so much
E.C.T. he thought his house in Cuba was in Kenya
and his second wife his first, his third some kind of matador.
I read about Nick Adams on the lake and all those
summer people first at Horton Bay and then in Paris and
Pamplona. They all said swell and I thought they were great
and even read the prose aloud. The names of places
that I knew myself would make me dizzy with the recognition
as I whisperingly incanted them in bed where I was often ill:
Petoskey, Charlevoix, Boyne Falls...

       If I knew these I might know Paris too
and even some swell girl who'd maybe show me her swell cunt,
a word that Scribners didn't let him print but that I knew anyway
from dirty-talking Nell on Hudson Street. We'd summer up in
Michigan on Walloon Lake like he did. At Shadow Trails Inn. I loved
my father then the way he had loved his, who taught
him how to fish and hunt before he lost his mind
and put a bullet in his brain. I think my father took the picture.
There I am holding up my bass.

II

It's now 2000 and we can't find Windemere. Thirty years
between his final summer here and 1950; fifty years
between my one big catch and this boat on the lake without a line.
Things have not been swell, have not been great.
Well, sometimes they were swell: a while ago, & in another country.
His phrases stuck forever in your mind provided that
you read him very young.

       But this week is okay. We've taken walks,
eaten whitefish both at Pippin's and the Walloon Inn,
and tried to figure what it means at sixty still to be alive.
Who at ten or twenty sees himself in forty, fifty years?
Robert Lowell barely made it; Berryman,
who sat cross-legged in my Salt Lake City room
and recited every word verbatim of *A Clean, Well-Lighted Place*
only got to fifty-eight. He said that story was a poem, and

he was right. I'm older than my teacher was
when he died. I'm older than Lowell. About the age
when Hemingway, who, like his father, like crazy Mr. B.,
knew he'd had enough.

                         I haven't had enough.
I'm greedy and want more. I like it here on this swell lake
and looking at the shoreline passing by like print
you scan searching for that great passage you can't find
but once had known by heart. The one that either
let you through into some other world or knocked you dead.

To read at all when I first read meant simply to read him.
Misogynist or drunk, vain & boastful & commercially
successful ruin like they say, he gave me passage anyway
to pass on by, forgetting & ungrateful. Now I have no interest
in those other houses on the shore, even in what's left of
Shadow Trails Inn, which all at once I locate from a bright
configuration of some oddly angling birches
that I haven't seen for fifty years. When we were here before
I didn't know about his cottage. Windemere.
He couldn't find it either until Paris when he'd lost it
in his life to win it for his art.
And then began to say that certain things were swell:
a lake, a girl, a morning catch of trout.
A clean well-lighted place was only clean and bright.

There's yet another photograph of everyone
at Shadow Trails Inn. Everyone but me, so this time
I was the photographer. Not a single person there was left alive.
Dick and Mary, John and Lois, Jim and Florence,
Cousin Nancy, Uncle Bob—there they were against a wall,
the flag up flapping on the pole. Some firing squad
from *In Our Time* must have come and shot them where they stood,
and there was nothing I or anyone could do.
It must have happened as I turned and looked away.

III

     Just how old
was Nico A. when he walked all dazed & drawn through Italy,
when he finally laid that girl in Horton Bay
having slain the others anyway with rugged looks and laughter.
(Lots of irresistible bad rhymes with Hemingway.)
My wife was Adams too (Diana) when we met in 1966.
She was swell & great & it was London & in May.

She points at something from the bow. A scene straight
out of *Gatsby* in a stately choreography
on someone's lawn. The swells are dressed in morning suits,
although it's afternoon, and pastel-colored gowns, tinkling ice cubes
in their glasses waiting for the host and hostess
circulating on the terrace, pitchers in both hands, to pour another Pimms.
The rich are different from the rest of us, said Scott.
They have bigger boats. Ours is maybe fifteen feet, plus outboard.
In a larger craft than this, I did in fact reach Paris.
Reached Pamplona, too. It's taken me a lifetime to prefer it here.
When I met Diana at some crazy Sixties party
she was standing at the far end of a narrow room and
looking like an advert for the mini-skirt. Was she
the cover-girl of that month's issue of *Time Out*
that featured "The Most Stunning Birds in London"?
(Birds of course were women who were swell.)
Men would stop & stare at her in the street. One man
wrecked his car, craning for a better look.
I couldn't believe my luck. And now she points again:
at naked swimmers in the lake, breast and buttock visible
with each new stroke, heading
from that Daisy of a dock across the lake to Eagle Point.

I like the old man's late erotic work. The things he couldn't
publish and kept working on in spite of hopeless odds
against completing them. Scribners held *The Garden of Eden*
for decades. How he loved the way those three, those
two birds and the guy, try things out he now could never do.
And even Nick and Littless seem intent on incest as they
light out for the territory half a mile from here while Mr. Packard

at the shop detains the wardens blathering about tobacco.
Left unfinished, Nick's last story stops at *Sure* when Littless
asks *And will you read it? Or is it too old to read out loud?*
Too old to read out loud? She's brought along *Wuthering Heights*.
Or did she mean Am *I* too old to ask you for this gift?
He'll read to her. It's swell, and so is she. She cuts her hair
like Catherine on the Côte d'Azur, calls herself a boy.
She says that they'll have children, swings her child's legs
astraddle on his hips. Sure, he says, I'll read.

He stops it there. His friend E.P. got back to Italy because
the rich old novelist could write him a swell check.
E.P.: who said to Lowell he'd started with a swollen head
to end with swollen feet. Hem, who measured Scott's
small cock & told him, Look: it only counts engorged with blood.

IV

The bodies of the dead lay all around him, drained
of blood, all engorged with gangrenous corruption. He thought
he'd lose his leg, and by the time he knew he wouldn't
was in love. The story is well known.
The facts as he reported them from time to time are questioned,
but the story is well known. It was Red Cross for sure
and not Italian infantry in which he served, but what the hell.
Some of what he said he did he didn't really do.
But he was born to tell a tale or two. They dug the shrapnel
from his leg and tore apart his knee to reassemble it.
He thought one night he felt his soul ascend out of his body
and return. His lady married, in the end, somebody else;
He came back here to heal…
                              We stopped in Horton Bay
to buy a paper at the general store. It seems to be
unchanged. The BBC had once brought in a film crew for a shoot
and asked the puzzled clerk: *Can we buy these?*
Presenting him a shopping list preserved for eighty years
scribbled out by Mrs. H., the doctor's wife.
They still sold everything except some kind of ghastly Spam.
Embarrassed that we only had a paper, I also

bought a bottle of Chablis. We've got it with us in the boat.
Was that the store where Mr. Packard had detained the wardens
letting Nick and Littless make their run?

The man next door at Red Fox Inn would know. He'll sell you
books or cook your lunch or put you up at night.
He's got the place declared a National Historic Site, and tells you
this is "Fox's House" in "Up in Michigan." Tempted
by a copy of *3 Stories & 10 Poems* which I had never seen, I
noticed it was Xeroxed in between the warping boards
he'd stitched and glued himself. He knew the canon like a Priest
his Bible, but he hadn't read or didn't like much else...
Mr. Faulkner? No. Mr. Fitz? A friend of Hem's. Mr. Joyce?
You mean that irksome Irishman? He'd made some maps with
marks and annotations noting where each incident occurred in all
the stories and he gave us free gummed labels saying
purchased from the heir of Volie Fox, fishing guru who taught
Hemingway his tricks. We stuck one on the bottle of Chablis.

He had my number, though, and shouted out *Goodbye Professor!*
and I turned about to say, *well actually I don't teach Him,*
but only waved, and thought of one old Brother in the Art, fired both
by and for his genius at my place of work, teaching even
Across the River to his Freshmen, saying of poor Cantwell,
If he could well he would well but he can't well.
The students, still too young to get it, laughed politely, none
of them as yet with serious wounds.
My friend was early wounded though he'd not been in a war.
He too left his shit and fluids in a hole he'd
dug in lethal earth which had not blessed him for his works.

V

Well, the perks of academia. That's why you are here
says my antagonist, some voice internalized
of Mr. Volie Fox. It's called a leave. It's a sabbatical.
Get off my gown. I'll gouge your eye out
with the corner of my mortarboard.
You're corrupt as all the rest, says Volie Fox,

even though you don't talk theory and you evidently
like to read. But you can't fish.
What you really go for is what Packard at his general store
tells his wife he hates: Chautauquas. You like culture.
You'd rather go to them than to revivals where
at least they get worked up and fuck each other afterwards.
Packard liked young Nick because he saw him swelling up
with original sin. This fishing boat's a kind of
water-slumming and you can't spend half an hour
on the lake without a book & wine…

And yet the water sometimes blesses even lubbers
and their books. The swells of southern seas, rivers, lakes, fjords
and even damned up creeks like one I played in near my house
on Old Glen Echo Drive. All water's amniotic, nowhere Lethe,
and we watch with joy those naked girls swimming
there some fifty yards in front of us like two fine porpoises before
a ship that's making for a landfall. On land you do fall down,
so any fool builds his house or city near the ocean,
or the river or the lake. Even bourgeois mother's sons from
Oak Park Illinois were close enough to smell
Lake Michigan in western winds and bend to its bravado.
Colonel Cantwell sans Viagra lay beside his girl
in Venice; in that gondola he knew she was the angel of death,
but rocked with her on the canal. And at the start
young Nick, whose lover called him Wemedge, heard
along with waves that lapped on shingle there at Horton Bay,
I love it, Wemedge. Love it. Wemedge, come.

Chautauquas came with Methodists & Women's Christian Temperance
to Petosky, where also Sherwood Anderson had lost his
scalp, burlesqued in *Torrents of Spring*. Packard who dislikes
Chautauquas also rails against "resorters," "change-of-lifers"
sitting on hotel front porches in their rocking chairs.
He must have been a friend of Volie Fox.
His wife on culture: "Packard, I won't bother you with this,
but it really makes me feel swell."
And on her change-of-life: "I'm still all the woman you can handle,
aren't I now"…

        We cut the outboard at the sand bar

and we open the Chablis. Still no sign of Windemere
that we can see. Diana points again. Unembarrassed, tall and brazen,
both the naked girls walk up on the sandy beach
and shake the water off their golden bodies like two dogs.
Then they turn to us and smile.

VI

He turns to her and smiles. Sure, he says,
he'll read. He'd meant before, I now remember, that the books
she'd brought were all too old for her, but he's
agreed to read one anyway, "out loud." That way, he
explains, it lasts a longer time. So when she asks
"Is it too old?" she means of course "for someone of my age."
But he's persuaded by this point and opens Brontë,
does the whole Chautauqua for the sister-boy on his knee.
In Salt Lake City J.B. said: Matthias, don't
read Proust until you're over forty—and so of course I started it
at once, looking, as we do, for secrets someone
thinks we shouldn't yet be privy to.

So there it ends in the selva oscura with *Wuthering Heights*,
the wardens having left the store & on their trail.
Which means he couldn't finish it, or was it really done?
Nights when I'm afraid and cannot sleep, Diana often says
Then shall I read? She means of course "out loud".
She knows that way it lasts a longer time. I always ask
for something that's too young for me, more likely
Pathfinder than Proust. It's what we have invented to
shut down my fear, send me off onto some quiet lake of peace.
She'll say, Some boy's adventure maybe?
How about your macho friend E.H.?
And I'll say, Adams, that's not fair! But I end up with
what I liked the best when I was twelve, & that was Adams
fishing here in Michigan. We don't do Heathcliff at Chautauqua;
we just troll on out for my one bass.

Although right now, awake, the outboard dead,
we do not have a line or pole or net.

You don't get bass or trout or marlin with your mind alone
(even if it conjures tigers in your bed).
We sit here rocking in the shallows, drinking wine.
The naked girls are gone. Shadows fall across
the party on the lawn. I am content.
But that's what Faust says when he's done for,
when he gazes on his works of reclamation in the hands of
that Chautauqua in apotheosis, old Herr G.
So things can be too Swell for our own good, swell
out of hand, grow cosmic in their folding
space right over into time. It's just the wine, my love,
the rocking on these waves, and it will pass.
This started out to be a poem about a bass I caught when
I was ten. And never once again.
You'll read to me tonight, I know. Whether Proust or
Mother Goose, it does its work. It's no big show
at the Chautauqua with a smell of gaslight, but it's exactly swell
enough, no more. It's great. In my life it's starting to get late.
We haven't yet found Windemere
and now the sun has set entirely on the lake.

My selections here are not chronological. Nor do they represent at all one important side of my work—long (and usually experimental) poems from "Poem in Three Parts" in my first book to "Kedging in Time" in my most recent. They also omit work from books available to me when the first *Five American Poets* anthology was published in 1979. This means in fact that my selections are taken from *Swimming at Midnight* (1995), *Pages* (2000), *New Selected Poems* (2004), and *Kedging* (2007). The reader will not find here much trace of my long sojourn in Britain, but poems from those days—1967–85—have been represented before on occasions similar to this one. I have taken some direction in the selections from responses of readers over the last couple of decades.

The opposite approach to the one I've taken would have been to print two long poems back to back—"A Compostella Diptych" from *A Gathering of Ways*, say, followed by "Automystifstical Plaice" from *Working Progress*, where a kind of modernism might have been encountered in a fierce embrace with a kind of postmodernism. Poems like these have their readers, and they establish one pole of a dialectic that I think has defined my development as a poet, such as it is. But that approach would constitute something more in the order of a statement than an introductory selection of poems inviting (one hopes some new) readers to become acquainted with a body of work that has both doors that open easily and windows that must be pried open with a crowbar. I apologize to those who enjoy coming in through the windows rather than the doors. I like going through a poet's windows myself. I have also been mindful to choose poems from my work that seem compatible with those of the other four poets.

This from an interview may be helpful.

JOE FRANCIS DOERR Robert Archambeau says in his preface to *Word Play Place* that his book of essays on your work focuses on the "fascinatingly arcane" rather than "refreshingly lucid" side of your work, in part because the less accessible poems require and reward more extensive commentary. Is there a problem that one might get a distorted sense of your career from the book?

JM   I don't think so. He's right that many of my shorter poems don't need to have much said about them. However, I'd like to think they could be "fascinatingly lucid" just as some of the more difficult pieces might be "refreshingly arcane." I've of course always written, and continue to write, poems of both kinds. In fact, the dialogue in my work seems to demand a poem of some simplicity and directness following completion of something oblique, allusive, and difficult. I followed "Automystifstical Plaice," perhaps the most extravagant poem I've ever written, with "Swell," a poem about sitting in a fishing boat with my wife on Walloon Lake in Michigan.

I especially like writers who have styles rather than a style. The story of our lives resists telling in a single mode as tenaciously as its meaning resists yielding to a single ideology. The composer Alfred Schnittke argued a case for "Polystylistics" at the Moscow Music Congress in 1971. In a poem about that, I find his position sympathetic.

> Serial and several, boys! When
> Menelaus asks for Proteus, he
> Knows the servant of Poseidon turns
> More tricks than Helen, and is
> Hard to hold. Plainsong stylized the
> Prayers: Singing at the monkish
> Hours of Prime, Sext, Nones, no one's
> Goods are Godly. Seals only barked
>
> One note to lost Achaeans. Steel as in
> Stalin pierced Shostakovich
> But not Schnittke...
>
> Even *In Memoriam* can waltz on broken
> Legs back from Leningrad to
> Old Vienna, even a quartet can play its
> Ending first and leap from Renaissance
>
> Orlando Lassus to the *Grosse Fuge*...
> Proteus may sing a pillar made of

Fire or water, but he sings. Stand to harms!
Poseidon at Apocalypse opens seven styles.

Yet setting off on any water, whether high seas or only Walloon Lake, a poet growing older, singing shanties in seven styles or only one, looks to his tackle and trim with care. I once called a rather optimistic book of poems *Crossing*. There it was all-ahead-full-steam and leave the boilers to the crew below decks; one hoped they didn't blow. A more recent book I've called *Kedging*. According to the *O.E.D.* and my own sailing experience, kedging is a way "to warp a ship, or move it from one position to another by winding in a hawser attached to a small anchor dropped at some distance." What pertains to the long title poem in that book might also pertain to the shorter poems in this anthology:

...what's the future of the future tense?
What's propitious in the past? Passing through the present
Kedging's all you're good for
With a foot of water under you, the tide gone out, the fog so thick
You can't see lights at Norderney but enter history in spite
Of that by sounding in its shallows with an oar.

John Matthias

JAMES MCMICHAEL

James McMichael's earlier books of poems include *The Lover's Familiar* (1978), *Four Good Things* (1980), *Each in a Place Apart* (1994) and *The World at Large* (1996). *Capacity* (2006), was a finalist for the National Book Award. He has received a Whiting Writers Award, the Arthur O. Rense Prize from the American Academy of Arts and Letters, the Shelley Memorial Prize and a Fellowship from the Academy of American Poets. He has written two books of prose, *The Style of the Short Poem* (1967) and *"Ulysses" and Justice* (1991). He teaches at the University of California, Irvine.

Pretty Blue Apron

0

In the separate histories
wanting writes,

zero doesn't count. Nothing had
happened yet. Zero.

Then it had. There was placental
discharge and infusion. These didn't

follow one another as the night the day,
there wasn't time. With nothing

private for it, undeprived,
the fetus took in everything as

one one one one one without one
"and" between,

without once knowing it was only one.
It got born alive and there one was,

1

a positive and whole number. Into
all one's chances, one unfolds

head first. God only knows the
start it gives one. One has toes.

Reaching for their lost water, each
wiggle of them squeezes through a one-way

pin-hole in time. It's too
much for one to tell that there's an

outside. The heart can't
swell any more toward it and

caves back in,
starts over into every ma–thump mortal

quaver it has left. For all one can
do about it, which is zero, one stays

2

proper to two. No two,
no one. There's second-person

fostering out there somewhere or one leaves.
Two could hardly

bear for one to have to go without.
Born to

see and be seen,
one sees two's face. Two

smiles as she nurses.
When the nipple slips away and isn't

there for awhile,
two's face is there. "There is" is

either of two's nipples, two's one face.
Between one's wanting and the two that gives,

there is a place for things to happen.
Is that look happening that one so wants?

To lack it takes up
one time: two looks, and it

arrives just at one's body at time two. All's
well again, until, again, pressed

forward so that now again, almost
before one lacks it, one's moved

out of the good. Where
is she, that good slaking mother? This one is

looking now again, that's better, good,
one's own smile shows in hers sent

back to one, and so on. After
long enough, there aren't

two mothers anymore, there's one whose
badness one says no to as one also says you

papa, you blue apron, you my lamb.

from *Each in a Place Apart*

            At school, I was a
squad-leader. I'd gotten enough votes. It meant
I'd wear as bandolier over my white T-shirt
a red cotton sash. It meant I'd say who'd play left field.
She was back in the hospital. My father saw her
every day. Though she was usually about the same,
tonight she was better. He took me to the
Crown Cafeteria, my favorite place to eat.
Waiting for the light so we could cross Colorado,
he said she'd died. The stairs to his office echoed.
Through the front windows we looked out over the street.
I was sitting in his lap in the big swivel chair.
    "But you said she was better."
    "She is better. This is better."

    The small, pretty woman at the station.
Where would she sit? Eager, tanned and brash, a soldier
followed her to the wide rear seat, I followed too but

stopped, tried not to listen, I was fourteen. Incredibly,
she moved. Could she sit with me? She was on her way
home from her sister's, she'd been there while her husband
closed things up in Fresno, where they'd lived before.
Did I like Utah? She did and didn't, and why.
My answers to her reasons spared me the tight
stultifying fear that I would touch her, her hand was
there but I wouldn't touch it, I could breathe, I managed
even to turn toward her when she talked. We went on to
families, mine first, her questions intimate and long.
She never betrayed it if she thought me young
but she wasn't flirting. I wasn't confused, I knew
right where I was with her: I was lost. It was getting
dark outside and we were hungry. We bought sandwiches in
St. George. Back on the bus, she said she hadn't
slept well the night before, I said she should put her
head on my shoulder if she wanted to. A quick pleased
hum in her throat as she skewed toward me, nestled,
and complied. Past Las Vegas, where she woke a little,
lifted it and then let it rest, her head
stayed on my shoulder. She slept. That was what mattered.
My vigil was to know that I could leave and not disturb her.
She held me just above the elbow with her left hand.
Wanting more and more to thank her and to say goodbye, I
knew she'd sleep beyond my stop and wake and think about me
mostly that I must have left.

       A highway runs the
length of the peninsula. The suburbs overlap.
She lived in one of them and took around with her
her setting. Shops and houses, luminous spring lawns,
streets that led off to places she'd speak French.
Unpunctured by the phrase "One evening" or "One fine day,"
her setting promised it would yield the longed-for.
We met one evening at church, but the adjacent
backyards, the balm of their untold repository
waiting in the dark as, introduced, we
looked at one another, looked away. 1964,
November, but the earth, its different settings for
still other stories, its planes of lines extending and
reversible at any point. Saltflats. An abandoned

Five American Poets

tinker's van in a swampy field. The wooded island
upstream from the bridge, the one down.

    Nor was it even then too late. I was the
married, reliable sponsor to her youth group,
I had to keep it to myself. Away from her, inside me,
it would suffocate, I thought, if I stayed busy.
My body kept it alive. What if she weren't
there again for a third straight week? I should
want her not to be there. Love meant wanting her to be
comely, prized and occupied, light-spirited, it meant
wanting her not to want me. Another Sunday and she
wasn't there. If I told her, would she want me then?
I couldn't tell her, couldn't not, and did.

    I wanted for her sake to undo it,
I asked her to forget. There wouldn't be
time for us since I was married. I'd made her want
another time, when, whole, impossibly together,
we'd rescue my avowal, which was a curse.
Though I asked her not to, she went on
waiting for that time and, by the tree where I
couldn't get away to meet her, waiting
undismayed, heartsick, eighteen.

    In my stupid arithmetic, we're
outnumbered, she and I, by my wife and two sons.
Barbara doesn't notice any change. We visit her
parents. Her dad and I go fishing. Bobby's in school.
Linda never asks me to leave them, never says she'll
leave me. We promise only that we'll meet next
week again at Vicki's or at Chuck's. The quick
assurances each time, we're fine, it's again been
less than too hard and here we are. Then always
rapture and protestation, doubt, self-doubt, and
lingering, the future that we're sure we've lost
forever there for us in our clothes on the cold floor.

    To get away from the house to see her
I'd kept pleading work. The library at school was
quieter, I'd said, the kids weren't there. It had served,

though they weren't troublesome or loud. Now, I sit them
next to one another, tell them I'll be moving
away for awhile, that I'm going to live
somewhere else. Nothing from Geoff, from Bobby
instantly a chuckle and smile.
    "Are you happy? Why did you laugh?"
    "Because now we won't bother you when you have to write."

    I have to teach again that fall and move back
down to Laguna. The days alone are less baleful,
they're just for a year. No one ever stops by,
but when she drives down on Thursdays after class
I meet her at the Tic-Toc Market. My apartment's
little more than the bed, and we can't wait.
Safe-harbored, whispering, with always more to tell,
we stay put, the dark catching up with us each week
until it's there in our first hour. From upstairs,
the muffled after-dinner clatter. Somebody's phone.
We start over at her knee, we're slower, the prolonged
fine sadnesses we'd hoarded from the years before
slow to give way and slowing so that only after
nothing for awhile does what we're doing take us
not toward her finishing again (or not right now) but
anywhere we've missed, her ribs, only the lightest
grazing of them, down and forward, not too far
nor too far back again across, each furrow
closer by its width to that last ridge below the pliant
dominating compass of her breast. We're being
pulled, of course. She hasn't stopped me. She won't.
At its outermost, her body's what she touches with.
It isn't long before she's moving too. Our skins
poised for the next just barely altered place, we're
thread-like stalks, light-running, sheer, our tiny leaves
flush with the basin's wide paved curb. It's still
gate-piered courtyard, ashlar dressed, a balustrade.
From jets above the circular pool alcoves,
water, its affection for an always lower point
tight-channeled in the iris rills, then underground,
the land dropping away through poplars to the dell.
Damp peaty banks easing to the full pond-hollow,
I'd never married, she'd been born to someone else.

Five American Poets

from *Four Good Things*

No sleep for either of us on the flight to
Maine and then to Gatwick. From the train, back yard
allotments and cooperatives, the city hardly
there at all outside Victoria and there inside it
only as a crowd. It's hot, of course, and everyone
just manages. We pass them in their queues. They need
maps and bookings, taxis, other trains. I try to think they
like some part of this. It would help me through the raw
worry of what to do if I could think they
liked it in some way I didn't. I ask about the
Grosvenor, and it's silly to have asked because it's
here, inside the station. We take our bags upstairs,
come down again, go out to look for dinner, eat,
come back and go to sleep. When I hear it, I know
first that it's coming from below, from that odd warm
hollow where the people were and where they must be now,
still purposeful and hearing differently this voice.
A woman's, young, it names in series all the single
destinations, platforms, times, then carries here with
nothing that disturbs me, nothing I can understand,
no word, with nothing lost, no listening and only
letting go, forgetting.

...To any number we can always add one
because it works that way, by adding numbers.
Because it's small, because our maps for it are much
larger than its surface, we've learned to print in
silicon, on chips, an integrated plane of
microchannels, spurs and gates. Its circuitry will run
twelve thousand operations in an inch,
the bits, with their addresses, there, inside,
not going very far. Because it remembers
perfectly, because it never sleeps, because it can
sort and compare and choose and find the proper
order in the sum of all its pulses, ON or OFF,
the things they say in eighteen million homes are
digitized and stored, revised, called up again by

GEOCODE with its coordinates for any point
P on the map, all references on grid and bearing
east and north in equal squares from their false origin.
We're somewhere in its mesh of cells and always
catching up. There's always, just ahead of us, a
rate or table, an estimate of trends that we
belong to and that waits. We watch it as we watch ourselves,
expectantly, afraid that in the calculus of
pain and pleasure, at the scale of 1:1, we're not
happy enough. To be happy, we have to be sure.
We'd be surer if enough of us were happy.
This many will kill themselves, this many won't,
or we'll be off a little in our reckoning.
As predicates of what's been well-rehearsed,
we're either well- or ill-behaved. To help us know
the different points of stress at different times, we're
averaged out, depicted from the top with all our
furnishings—and there are scripts. The stir at breakfast.
Sandwiches are being cut. We see how much room
Mother needs at the work-top when someone else
passes behind her with a tray. The toddler wanders
in and out of the kitchen as she tidies up. She's
bathing him now, lifting him from the tub: is the floor
wide enough here for her to towel him dry?
We need our clearances and kinds of peace from
sideboards and chairs, settees, rectangular or round
coffee tables. They steady us, these things we've made.
We move between them, retrieve a sameness from the same
bookcase, the same clock. People don't always want to
watch TV when it's on. They need a place to sit
away from it so they can talk or read. And in the
bedroom? Should they try it with more pillows?
Standing up? What is it that might singularly
please them there as they imagine it being
better than the last time, than the best?
Is it how she'd seem to know before he asked,
or that her breathing as she came would take him too?
In the quantum of their parts and how they move,
where are they when they've started? His cock's
inside her and they've started, her labia

just visible around him on the outward strokes.
It troubles us that we don't quite see to the
heart of a place. Whatever shows itself
conceals its other sides and how it works.
She's leaning on her hands, astride him, her face
strained and turned away as, in and out, more
surely now, he feels her start to ease beyond this
time they're keeping. He tries to slow her but she's
past it, past her wanting. And as she comes,
it's like the wakefulness she leaves when he's been
holding her and waiting and her shudder tells him
now, now she's asleep, she's left him, and he comes.
Equal, complete, their bodies are as far away as
outer is from inner, then from now. As if for
each of them inside their separate minds
there was another who was listening to them think,
they're not so much alone as by themselves.
They're thinking. Neither speaks. Infinity being a
funny number, we lose them to themselves as each
remembers and awaits, concurrently, from
anywhere in time and nowhere yet, another
part of what they're thinking or a pause.

…Along the boulevards, in 1840, the flâneur
chatted with whom he pleased as casually as the
pace his turtle set him. I try to imagine him
subtler than that. Although he'd talk with them sometimes,
they'd rarely place him by the way he dressed
or by his preference for districts. Letting the crowd
inscribe him with its hurry and its looks,
he'd be its marker, watching—it would be by
him that we might figure who we are.
Disdainful, and preoccupied, and tired,
it's what we miss that makes us passers-by.
I meet someone. We talk. We're both a little
surprised that it's that easy. Am I sounding
too cordial, too relieved? It isn't
traveling that makes me ask. I do the same thing here.
I think too much beyond my part in what I'm saying.
Is this other person interested? I can't be sure.

James McMichael

To shame me out of wanting to be sure,
you've told me that you think I'd feel more
interesting if I were dying. That just might
do it, you think. It might me remind me more that
I'm interested, me. I wouldn't lean so far
ahead of myself, I wouldn't have to,
I'd have my closure with me as I talked.
Maybe it's what I want. I hope you're wrong.
I still might ask you "Have I told you this before?"
We tell each other things that are only
starting to make sense. If they seem to make
more as we tell them, and if we go on,
what is it that we're leaving out? We're past it now.
Whatever it was, we didn't have to say it, didn't
break with it in the way that talking breaks
open, within it, between its parts, a time for
other parts, intrusions, more chances to be
missing what we meant to say. Linda was
awake one night and wanted to tell me where she'd
gone with them that afternoon. They'd parked at a
power station, where it was flat. There were tracks
already for their skis and they skied there until
Giorgio or Pironda thought they should go around
behind the village by some poplars and try it up
that way. The buildings thinned out and there were
sheds with animals with piles of straw outside and
men in some of the sheds and outside too with more
straw for the animals and bringing out the dung.
She had to go around bushes and small trees. She kept
falling, and they all laughed and decided to come
back through the village because it might be easier.
The street was ice and hardly wide enough for
two of them at a time, or for a cart.
They felt showy in their bright nylon.
A woman with a bowl looked at them from her door.
Chickens. A covered water-trough. She told me
more about the street and then remembered.
What she was saying, she said, was that there were
farmers out working in the snow.

The British Countryside in Pictures

          The frontispiece fixes as
British
a man whose
livelihood is the grass. As he had

before the take and
since,

he plies away in the sun.

"Market Day."
Storefront awnings slope into the square.
Among the occupied,
only the vendors are without hats.
Well–fatted,

sweet and full of pickle are the hooked gibbets of
beef above the pens.
The plate after

"Tractors on Parade" is untitled.
Where the village high street's

walls converge at the far end,
a motor-car has entered and parked.
Pictured empty in another,
the new Great West Road has working

fields to either side. In the one format,

affordable and bound print by print,
grass advances as a factor
never to be run out of by a

people at home.
The farmer is to be seen as having at last put
dearth right.
Nature was on its
own side always. Necessary

against nature sometimes to forbear from making
more mouths to feed.
With the poorest twelfth begetting
half the nation,

the interests of soil and
race were served
by the politics of the straight furrow.

In the countryside
alone it was that one was spared meeting

the less right sort of girl.
Need.
It had become at last what only
others knew,
even if they were in one's midst.

Outside in

Kenya,
Madras,
Shaanxi,

Quixeramobim,
nature had put in place
disastrous shortfalls,
need and epidemic,
nature had played out

Ireland again.
Of those invisible millions who were gone,

nothing was missing.

Nothing was missing
for them. There without need,
they were the revenant in England's garden,
they were the ones whose absence is their sign.

Of the unperceived who keep
safehold where they hide,

vision is a forgetting.
The British were those whom nature let bring home
as graveclothes to the ones its starved

arboreal and floral plantings.
England was green.
There belonged
ill-matched to many their likely

allotments of soil.
Across the range of them from
kitchen-gardens to pleasance,
these were not brandished. They were kept up.
While there were throwback native

cottagers who grew potatoes,

a weekly show on
gardening was aired.
All crystal sets picked up the BBC.

Because those grounds least frequented
were grounds where need was least,

of most
avail was a garden if
no one was there.
The walled reserve was model.
Its expert and only

viewers were staff.

What showed above the fine clean tilth was
surplus.
From its abounding
beds each day,

staff saw to it
for one:
by the garden's having made an
excess of nature,
nature was trumped.

Need had been made less natural.
Replaced was the old
productive ideal that the useful

good was desired.

The desired good was
useful in the new ideal.

Things become useless in the hoarding of them.
Needed for a nation's
surfeit of goods were buyers
primed by their wanting. Desire's

deputy
was the person in love.
An appetite need not slacken if what one

craves is the scarce,
and there is but the one beloved

only.
No hunger
feeds so on itself
as being able
never to have one's fill of someone prized.

They had become friends.

It would not have
occurred to him that she did not
love him. Of

course she did.
Friends love one another.
It began to explain his finding now that
along with love she also

gives him desire. Under something the
sway of which is undue,
in love with her,
he learns that he has had cleared
inside him

a constructed

garden-like place.
He practices his absence

as the stilled reflecting surface of its pool.
With features of her person in his
stead there,
to what is not its

own anymore in wanting

the self is sent
back by the other.
Far enough beyond
reason already is any
one such transport. Improbable

twice over
that with the same conclusive keenness

she should want him.
He looks for cues that
he too had given

her desire.
They are not there.
There is the coming
war to think of as well.
With conscription on its way,

better to be no more than
genial with her for now.
That is why it is her
suitcases he reaches for when he

meets her at the St Pancras train.
Right from the start he is off ahead of her
efficiently down the platform.

Against him from behind,
her fingers have it in them

that she will have to break away

too soon again for her return north.
Out of her greeting hand on his
back he walks.
For no longer than withdrawal

itself takes,
her touch had been there.

Wondering at its light
circumspect grace,
he does not mistake its bidding. What
she wants
he can from this time on want

for her. There can be no

help for them now since what
she wants is him.
Made nearly

bearable by desire is one's not being able to
withstand the desired.
The hurried meetings follow.
Their wanting one another comes to take on
greed as its base.

From the next moment between them
least likely to be surpassed
they carry
away from one another into their days away

more wanting.
It will be weeks.
To be with her

through them instead. If they could be already
beyond the war and

years on,

they might have lives.
Whole patches of days would have to be
discordant, humdrum.
Rote would help them through.

Given ordinary times to

lift her from,
have her lift him,
he would have come to

preside with her over their chances. Around them
everywhere was the petition that

dailiness might hold its gracious own.
Toward it came
sandbags on the corner pavements.
Post-office pillar-boxes were rigged with
gas-detecting paint.

The mask itself smelled of rubber. What one saw

first through its eyeshield was one's own
canister snout.
Leaflets from the Lord Privy
Seal's Office were

"Evacuation: Why and How"
and "If the Invader Comes."
So the enemy might

lose themselves in their confusion, the stations'
signposts came down. There were now
barrage balloons overhead
and searchlights.
The Anderson shelter was

corrugated steel.
It needed a garden to be sunk in.

Two million more acres were to come under the plough.
Collected for their great trek
out of the city,
the children walked

"crocodile" to the trains,
a loudspeaker telling them
"Don't play with the doors and
windows, if you don't mind, thank you."
Villages and towns were to accept a number

equal to their populations.
Each child had a printed label.

Each was allowed one toy.
They were met at the other end
by strangers who had come to

see who they were.

A lady with a clipboard sought billets for them
Some of them were in tatters.
The more doleful were often the last picked.
This was to be where they would
live now for a time,

out here in the country.
Files of them traipsed the lanes behind their teachers.
They were shown how to strip
hopbines,

how to make rush baskets out of reeds.
Boys served as beaters for the pheasant-shoots.
Harvest of course meant that

sheaves had to be carted. The sturdier of

both sexes
were put to work in the fields.

No bombs fell into the warm, beautiful autumn.
Most of the children went back home.
When it was time to
leave again for the country,

few of them did.

Above the blackouts,
the Germans were led at first by
moonlight up the Thames estuary.
Then it was by the fires.
Sounding like

stones being thrown at the front wall,
the incendiaries melted steel.

Bombs that screamed their way into the city
thudded down.
A smell of cordite followed.

Looked to be needed each month
were twenty million feet of seasoned
coffin-timber. There were
no more blue waterproof bags.
With the raids coming every night but one,

the dead might have to be dumped in the channel.

It is in bodies given to be seen that
ghosts meet their term.
Their transparency is no less restive.

Escapes that would fail are
patent already

in the pre-war countryside exposed.
Phantom in a picture are gaps that might have been
filled by a child.
One plate is called

"A Quiet Corner."

A trading-wherry is about to tie up.
Full sunlight has
to itself again for the afternoon
the bench
an East End child had jumped from for her

sprint to the canal. She had seen that
ropes needed securing. Having
called to her up the slope,
the bargeman was mindful that at

that same lock last spring
a man had asked to take his picture.

There are pollarded
willows in the picture. In another,
a hedge-crowned wall.

Stills of the countryside are composures.
They apply to keeping
outcome at bay.
Nameable,

all finite things are
present to one another for as
long as they show.
The bedding planes first. Ready
never to be seen as country,

they are exposed sometimes as its side.
On show in their single plots,
slate, shale and

weald clay,

marl,
the Tertiaries,

chalk and upper greensand.
A former seafloor laid down
shell by shell,

limestone dislikes interruption.
As stuffs from its lighter understories wear away,
streams take their sources back
farther with them into the scarp.
The cap-rock

outliers they leave are often wooded.
Sight is of the senses

the one that most
lends itself to remove.
Each prospect for the looker-on is
his without trespass.

Across the tiers of houserows up from the river,

each profile shows what its volume
stretches to from its
mid-point out.
The ridges to their backs are in cloud
where the sheep pass

down from high summer grazing.
Their drove-road takes the turn of the hill.
Inviting the indicative,
the tie-bulwarked lawn above it has its

copy in the millpond's glaze.
Another figure appears who speaks English.
Upfield from the crude railing over a footbridge,

his alternately-forward

knees are caught
mid-stride.

Above the Red Deep-Water Clays

   Capacity is both how
much a thing holds and how
much it can do. From a solid
magnetized and very hot core, the earth

suffers itself to be turned outside.
Closest to its heart are the deepest submarine
trenches and sinks. Its lava finds

clefts there in the old uplifted crust,
the ocean floor a scramble. Wrapping at depth huge

shield volcanoes, the North Atlantic

down- and upwells, its denser layers making
room behind them through the blue-green shortest
wavelengths of light. Inside the cubic
yards it levies,
league by league, respiring, budgeting its heat,

it hides its
samenesses of composition through and through.

For the normal water level,
an ideal
solitary wave is surplus. Any wave's

speed is what it is
only if reversing it would render it still.
Surfaces are almost without feature
at Sea Disturbance number one.

When the wind stretches them, their wrinkling gives it
more to hold on to. Three is
multiplying whitecaps.
Spray blows in well-marked streaks at six.
In the foam-spewed rolling swell that takes a

higher number,

small and medium
ships may be lost to view for a long time.
Waves are additive. Doming

up on the tidal bulge into a storm's
barometric low,
the distances between them widen
as from the Iceland-Faeroes massif

leeward for another
three hundred miles southeast

they build unblocked. Little

enough for them
the first outlying gabbro
islets and stacks. These are not yet THE BRITISH
COUNTRYSIDE IN PICTURES, not yet the shoals
off Arran in the Firth of Clyde.

Posited

   That as all parts of it
agree in their low resistance to flow,

so should it be agreed to call it water.
To say of water that it floods both
forward and back through places
difficult to place demands that the ensouled

themselves make places for their parts of speech,
the predicates arrayed in
front of or behind the stated subject—

water, in the case at hand. Water

attains to its names because it shows as one thing
speech is about.
It shows as water.
To say no
more than that about however broad a sea is

plural already,
it says there must be something

else somewhere,
some second thing at least, or why say
how the thing shows? Before it can be taken

as a thing, as sea,
there have to have been readied for it other
possible-if-then-denied pronouncements—land,
the sky. Possible that
somewhere in the midst of waters there could

be such things as might be walked on,

hornblende and
felsite, quartzite, remnant
raised beach platforms, shales,
a cliff-foot scree.

Until given back accountably as
extant and encountered,
nothing counts. Nothing counts until
by reason it is brought to stand still.
Country. That it stands over

against one stands to reason. Not without
reason is it said of country that it
counters one's feet. To count as

groundwork for a claim about the ground,

reason must equate with country.
To be claimed as that, as country,
sand blown inland from the dunes must
equal its having landed grain by grain.

All grains have their whereabouts.
From emplacements in their clumps of

marram grass and sedges, some will be
aloft again and lime-rich
grain by grain will land.

Country is its mix of goings-on.
For these to tally, befores from
afters must at every turn divide.
Before it turns,
a cartwheel has its place to start from. It

stands there in place. In place an
axle's width away, another

parallel wheel is standing.
Not for long.
After each wheel in concert leaves its
first place for a second,

it leaves again at once a third and more. No more nor

fewer are its places on the strand that it has
time for in its turning.
Imprinted
one at a time,
these places are the lines the cart

makes longer at each landward place.
Not late for what goes

on there as its heft at each next place bears
down onto the loams and breaks them,
the seaweed-laden

cart is in time. Time is the cart's

enclosure. There for the taking, time is
around the cart,
which takes it from inside. Around
stones in the dry-stone dyke are

times out of mind,
those times the stones' embeddings let them go.
The hill-grazings
also are in time, and the three cows.
The blacklands are in time with their

ridged and dressed short rows of barley.
As it does around

bursts that for the places burst upon
abandon where they were before,
time holds around

the moving and the resting things.

Back

>   A place can be disposed so
> ill toward them that many
> lives are untimely.
> To a nation by one's
> birth to it belongs the law to carry
>
> through to their ruin
> all untimely lives.
>
> Securing to it through their mothers' travail
> all bodies that can make do,
> capacity stays
> ahead of what happens,
>
> it fits it
>
> out for them first that they might
> feed and pass waste.
> A first thing the neonate
>
> mouth had been for in hunger was to seize.
> Emerged from,
>
> its capacity to
> be what it was had not yet
> fallen away to the later
> moves it would make to
> fix it,
>
> the mouth did
> not yet have words.
> There were the folds of
>
> lips around it and
> cheeks,
> the baby hull from the throat down
> walled in its scarfskin film,

the cells

flattened now without their water.
The brain itself the skin was of a
piece with already.
Soon enough,
it would have to be for more,

would have to consign
inside,
as through the tissue behind it,

each lambent trace.
Only this first once had that perhaps not been a

must yet.

A person
starts out and lives. One moment
on from that start—
still breathing and imperfected,

still in the way—
the body has regards that

tell upon it.

A person goes on being led to find as
looked-for
the things in his ken. There are
items there.
These guard against his being

nowhere at all.
If being was at first not
yet for the body
the entities that had

made their ways there,
not yet was the light of day
a showing only.

Five American Poets

Though finite
beings were there with the needful
spacing between,
the light they showed in also hid
their infinite remove from how they might

never in fact have showed.
The spacing

itself showed.
Of the newborn only one
moment before,

it was all that had showed.

The allotted
spacing,
the room,
the nothing–there: so

stretched had it been
eventually
that it was

his to break through.
Just given

outlet to,

he was perhaps still
of the nothing–there at
advent for that
first blink only,

nothing
alone it may have been
that skin was pulled
back to at first.
There was a nothing of his

own now.
It was accommodating,

this room his inner
parts took for
what they might do.

For a body's holding-parts to be
arrived at and hold,
their spacing must from the first be drawn out as much
forward as
back.

From then on more and

more it is to their one last turn
that by their drivenness
they fill and empty.
The cerebellum will in time

expand. There as its
bent already in the size alone
will be its drive

away from the short-lived body.
Much that is
not drive
ranges there
outside. Into it

forward from the body's organs as
against the outside will be

prostheses,
place-holdings
added to the body's destined place.
Some are there early.

Tall,

heavy, charged and
white on the low horizon,
a block print of clouds
breasting the rain-cleared air will be at
hand for the child in

MOTHER GOOSE.
While there will have been
sons in both theaters who had
not come home,

ready as well will be
the slots and tabs of wooden

jig-saw pieces for

"An English Cottage Garden,"
the border intact by the first
Christmas after

WWII.
Inside a backyard
tent at night,
not knowing where the

sky stops will be enough the same as

knowing he will die.
Executive,

one's being
implements its own completion.
One's call from the start

is from ahead where there is nothing.
The body in
Advance thus always of what a person
in itself
is,

it shows along the way as having not yet

done what it must. To have
done with it at last means
no relation, not

air anymore,
not heat, no tonic
likelihood nor interval,
no remnant,

nothing to see.
Being is what there is
when beings that had come to light are
no longer there.
Being quenches itself on its

out-of-this-world pull forward.
Against the end itself if also

from it,
craven,
false,

the imagined turnaround

backward in time.
He could
retrace in reverse each
percept, act and wish that had
made up his life,

each one could be discarded, he could
think it away.

When one tends back,
it can be thought to have happened
first for a little
that the body held becalmed from before it was born

the give-and-take

fondling of its begetters,
that ruffle they had left it in its
being made.
To caress means to go
on to what end,

what reason
ever would there be to stop
when still on call
beyond the place one reaches toward

lie other skin and
progeny,

how many in the line descending would it
ever be enough to
quit with just there?

Becalmed outside on the nascent
body perhaps
once only was a
first light graze.
With the nerves inside perhaps at

rest still if
poised,

it had become as well in less than
no time at all
the last
least trifling

ever to be let pass.
Skin had not yet had to have a
back to it.

Paper-thin,

it had happened to have been brushed.
Outside the mother's
aperture now,
so much for the dark.

Since Beginning
itself begins the one death one is
born toward
and will not bear,
the light was

again at once

closed over. Closed over at
once in the opening was every

other look
the skin might have had.
When cleared of that first

flutter across it was the newly
brought-to-light skin,
the shift to its
second light had been
too quick to see.

In the run at once
into it and then

on,

the first could not now be gone
back to.
Back would from then on have to be

a light made fast.
Sizings of
egg white had been spread on single sheets with
citric acid,

salt and silver nitrate.
Cameras for a century

had held the gel inside in

just the right place.
1946. From halide
grays that had taken
eight years before,

fine black and white points neighbor
end to end across
each of the several hundred,

THE BRITISH COUNTRYSIDE IN PICTURES,
a book of photographs in green
flexible boards.
So little too
early for him are these likenesses that it will be

months only
before he is born to die.
Tucked around that moment back into his
absence in the pictures,

he is reconceived.

His body having not yet
differed from it,

any one scene's plenty is his
death-mask inverted.
Reversible to the eye
the path above the foreground yarrow and gate,
a plough-team in the middle distance.

The span by span erasure of him
spectral there
inside the picture's

outside-of-time
safe spatial harbor,

he is in repeal,
exempt,
the coppice to the left behind the rise
a boyhood haunt.

The Believed In

  Christmas comes from stories.
These promise that God's love for us will outstrip death.
Only if it's not likely to can the believed in happen.
All I can be sure of waiting for it
is that I want it to come. Than almost anything,

I'd rather it be love that at its last the body can't

take anymore and dies of,
alive at once to its having been made good.
Results at the end vary. Children beloved by them
are sometimes told by the dying

"I thought it would be you of
all people who would keep me here."
If it's to be to God's keep that I give up those I lose,

then God both knew what it was to lose a son and could do
nothing either time to save him.

That doesn't sound like God. I'm supposing God can do all.
Lost twice to body, Jesus was as quickly back again in
God's love forever.
It was given to me to have been

loved for my first six years in a house that had my nanny
Florence in it and my mother and dad. Never talked about
even by them,
my mother's doom was there too. In the looks those three passed,
each had to have seen the stakes in who was who

and may have wanted to switch.

I'm lost to the ways that love is right
at bodies sometimes, always just as it's leaving and
often without touch.

AFTERWORD

I wish I'd instead said something extraordinary when I left
infancy, but the first phrase out of my mouth was "pretty blue
apron." The poem by that title refers to my personal history as a
fetus, a newborn and a toddler. That history is brought forward
chronologically in the poems that follow it. Along the way, a
wider view of the world presents itself until, in the last two poems
of the selection above, there's a return first (in "Back") to the
moment of my birth and then (at the end of "The Believed In")
to a summary of my first six years.

By that time, I had an addiction to the radio. It must have
started with my parents' interest in Fred Allen, *Duffy's Tavern*
("Where the elite meet to eat"), Jack Benny, Burns and Allen,
Bob Hope, *One Man's Family* and, in the winter, the Nightly
Frost-Warnings. There was a piano in our little house which I
picked at with my right hand, one note at a time. I was in the
Boys' Choir at the Pasadena Presbyterian Church, which was a
gothic shell, had good organists, and, before I left, a preacher
named Ganse Little, whom I wishfully misremembered as having
been there sooner than I've come to learn he was. My favorite
parts of the services book-ended by Bach were his sermons. From
the first time I heard him, I was intrigued by his deftness in
moving from one matter to another without at any point letting
the import of what he was telling us fall through the seams.

By the time I was twelve, I had a paper-route that paid me
enough to buy Benny Goodman's Carnegie Hall Concert, live
and studio recordings by Stan Getz, Bud Powell, Charlie Parker,
Art Pepper, Lee Konitz (still only early, pre-Wayne Shorter),
Miles Davis, and Lenny Tristano. It wasn't until the seventies that
Beethoven and Mahler got hold of me for good.

In college at the University of California Santa Barbara, books
whose followable sense would otherwise have eluded me were
opened and enlarged by my teachers: Benjamin Sankey, Homer
Swander, Marvin Mudrick, Hugh Kenner, and Edgar Bowers.
Bowers had been Yvor Winters' student, and it was at his sugges-

tion that I applied to Stanford. At the end of my four years there, I suspected, correctly, that I wouldn't again in my life learn as much as I had there from conversations with peers.

Hazard Adams hired me in 1965 for the job I have today. To him I owe a great deal, most of all the time I've needed to write what I've written.

James McMichael

JOHN PECK

John Peck was born in Pittsburgh in 1941, and raised there and in Cambridge Springs, Pennsylvania. He received his BA in English from Allegheny College (overlapping there with Richard Pevear), and gained a PhD in English and American Literatures at Stanford University in 1973, and a diploma in analytical psychology at the C.G. Jung Institut in Zurich in 1992. In 1978 he was awarded the Prix de Rome and spent a year as a fellow of the American Academy in Rome. Between 1968 and 1970 he counseled applicants for Conscientious Objector status. He has taught literature and writing at Princeton University, Mount Holyoke College, the University of Zurich, and briefly at Skidmore College and MIT. Since 1992 he has been in private practice as a Jungian analyst in Vermont, Massachusetts, and Connecticut, and as a freelance translator and editor.

Viaticum

Shedding ravines
And mist shoaling the cirques
What we were has come with us
What we are hangs back
The sky waits for its thunder

Padded sticks at the temples
Our only rhythm
Then our guides calling
Small wishbones caught in their mouths
Gill pulse through a pine wind
That sucks at lichens and our names

Next they will raise their arms
To the last cols
Doors in this termless morning
Sills, thresholds
And the firmness beyond

And then we too can shout back
Towards the windlost faces
Ears waiting
Through involved porches and the blood within
Beachless interior
River and drum

Dust runs after the deer
Cloud prints the mountain

Letting Up

The meander of my walking, and through it
A sun that swings to go with me at each turn,
And sweet fatigue that remains childlike because
    It works at nothing.

Push aggressively enough at the stout weave
Of what is, appearances we must take as
Being at least what they seem, and you tear through,
    You come stumbling out

Where the bright warmth sealed behind late windows seems
Miniature tenderness and stale fury, seems
To dwindle with cold speed as feet find themselves
    Running now, fleeing,

Carrying a stick figure who cannot let up.
This, too, comes to me from my walking, the one
Map of it that I have, unrolling between
    One step and the next.

When the gray infantry broke through at Shiloh
They found campfires, skillets over them cooking,
Sunday breakfasts laid out, and swirls of steam still
    Coming off coffee.

Communion that seems an end, fleeting, factive,
Must begin somewhere. They stopped, ate and drank, snooped
Through tents and read letters from girls. And they were
    Lost to the advance.

Hazelnut

Instead of perfectly evading us
the power swole and burst like a hazelnut
set in the fire, all the while holding shape
in his mind, as he wrote to his father Leopold.
So it can be. And so then came the unfolding
through sketches during the hot carriage rides
towards after-dinner card tables, the Prinzessin's,
to improvise among the unhearing. But once
the Landgrave set down his ivory toothpick,
staring at nothing, taken by the modulations,
the fragrant stink from his ceramic pipe
in trilling swirls, the musketry at Salzburg
and Amalia's hair long ago. Those also
smolder, also delay within the broadcast
efflorescence not wholly held in score
or serially decaying minds of those seated
in curved rows to listen, there or here
or in future, no more than in one stab
of the sky zigging down between cool firs
rimming the slopes he scanned from the swung carriage,
he has been telling me one thing all this while,
or in reedy whine of shrapnel off stone
at the bend of that road when another brain flared out
to sink like his unregistered in the field,
hearing—it enters between the shoulder blades—the river
of cloudy light, wet granite, and starmoss dirt.

Wind under Sash, Val Ferret

Night-stuttering glass, a brisk hexameter
   as if the shade of Rudolf Borchardt passed
self-refugeed again, not singular in that honor
     yet alone out there,

   carrying on his back the evening purples of the Mantuan
     and the ladder cliffs of Alighieri
back into Italy, back into the disheveled, shaken
     atelier of the villa,

   not as gods in his rucksack, nor the images of gods,
     not as *lares* but as the icons of men
carrying them, themselves carriers—for the clouds
     raked by the peaks

   admitted only the most portable pieties
     and promised cyclone over anti-cyclone
of our new rain, saint clown seer duke *bona fides*
     of the types of the peoples,

   amazon skull-smasher demoniacal berserker
     social democratic emperor
sculptor manipulator-of-masses-in-bulk worker
     plunging to the far plain,

   paladin pastor pathfinder toppled out of the human
     to the primaries of a pre-world—
but trekking down, there was a German and a man,
     his paces still spacing them.

    As if the shade of Borchardt rattled the sash:
even before the fist of the subjugator could squeeze him
    onto the roads, he numbered the hands
to be hacked off, and went, not giving in to his doubt
     that the rope he would rappel onto

might have been jerry-rigged over that jumble down there...
    and in that moment let me suspend him
as the fist of the folk did, not alone though singular,
      rhizome dangling in the unrooted.

Leaving the Central Station

    Now that my own was moving,
now that change was sliding in, quickening,
faces on the platform hinted things
striving to show themselves, to touch the fact
of weight unmooring into vague futures, blank—
but then I sat up and turned: *Haydn!* a sharp pull,
not the face but the fact of Haydn, that tug
part of the speed, colors beginning to run,
spreading out to take the name, now, *Mozart!*
and it was no face in particular,
with sweeping granites of the retaining wall,
rushing bright oblongs for cigarettes, beer,
and scraggles of dry vine dangling between them,
militiamen under packs, bowed slightly
by their dark rifles, with two last children,
girl running a tight circle around boy,
a pressure no sooner stated than developed
spirally, crumpling funnel in the chest
engulfing those close strangers
                settling back
into themselves and reaching for something to read,
pale in plate glass we were forms for that pouring
and its planetary, nostalgic clatter,
with the two gentlemen and their activity
not gone therefore although left quite behind
dispersed and swirling, submerged after being found,
turning to the next idea and its pursuit,
going off separately though they knew each other,
deposited back there or below, each of them
humming and churning, while apartment blocks
thin and scatter and raw fields open out.

Interleaved Lines on Jephthah and his Daughter

Lawn at sunset, during arrival, before the visit,
    for having returned in pride the general turned father,
not a field for crossing, bladed with amethyst,
    greeted with fulfillment, when the voice sailing out
and crisp withies of hazel twisting through hawthorn
    was his own girl's as she ran towards him. No, not thee.
lithe and strict, that gate of a green power.
    His pledge to victory was the first who should leap the sill.
For the invitation is to bring gifts to the feast
    the face of battle newly unveiled itself as hers,
though they could not yet pass the shadowing door,
    and the face of submission as the new face of battle.
Green at evening is drenched with the price and the consequence.
    for what should he do in some other place, with less wagered?
Emerald is not heartless, but a sunk tide of fire,
    and some other conquest, such could never be his,
jade is the pomegranate turned away, speeding past harvest.
    More than readiness unfolds the eddying sun,
unwithheld, unknotting against the remainder,
    not alone while it revolves there, nor unseen.

Times Passing the Breakwater

    Intimate address
    imperial and addictive
    will move to annex experience
    it glimpses but hasn't had—
    and so, before our beginning, Termia,
    before the claimed but unsurveyed
    territory of your hair
    parted across those decades, their cold neck
    sleeving a hot throat and dark speech,
    even then, as if you had been there,
    my arm swept out in a wide gesture

to net the starched jibs
tacking and crossing—

hand isolated
in the sealed car as that mass smoothly
shot the stone causeway
in its groove of force.

At indigestible speed
Ezekiel converged
with the ballistic pellet, rolled grief word
dropped on his tongue, and swallowed.

Medicine, too, for the contained!
Distributed along the urgent
metabolic fuse, into
imploded strophe and dispersed canzone.

Ignorant, what I'd assumed
but not wholly dreamed
was this: possibility as a body
naked, ageless, taking into itself
containment without limit,
curled in on itself unborn
yet with breasts gathered full to the knees
and its hands merged in devout cutwater, hair
pouring forward from the accepting nape:
emblem germinal and creedal
with the sun over it unzoned,
hills and shores streaming into it
from a lifetime unbracketed—
each station of our going,
boats and their bright rowers hailed
as companions, the stranger
waving back…
that much came clear
as it floated off, lifting into view
even as it dissipated.

You had more on your mind:
through noon's bland core you were to stitch lightnings,
bread of Zechariah through his speared tongue,
the word of power like his bomber
planing in for its run.

One day, and one hour
threading the strict eye
of its incalculable instant.
Road by the sea.

★

From a late hearth
one spark, the aimed remnant,
gashes high through the gulf
its hypnotism of space, as desire
would dodge past morning: it has the flight
without the passage.

Neither as one thought
nor as two such, separate,
but as one contradiction
tensing to complete its arc limit,
we were taken up, were held
in one act of attention,
sputtering weld extinguishing first
one flux and then another
in the torch's mute issue,
and how long it bore
or at what frail height it quenched in a surf headlong
I cannot gauge.
     The crest highway
streams with paired humming tracers,
and closed on itself the eye spins
their homing fire, draining,
until there is only the crew from yesterday's boat
spreading their nets along
the inlet, turning to inspect
cloud where it fumed up, squiggle
on the last high cast of light:

it is they, instinctively, who'll have drawn
some inference. One mind
and the turn seaward, crabs
pulsing through drenched sand.

★

Daybreak vapors swift poles past the train's tremor—
slow strobe through wet glass into the stiff skull.
Your terms are not yet those of she who saves,
gentler though terrible, surer,
able to say she'll return
to the light she came from, whereas
your endings extend codas through echoes, leading
down the labyrinth.
     The signalman
coming off his last shift wades
his tide of returning self,
the numbed powers. What he hid
in the world was his effort,
hid with the unsaid and the relinquished,
his rhythm now their seal. Lodging it there,
he has not lost it.
    But your manic
scribes bend over its fluid map—
you gag the throated rememberer and inspire
interpreters, as if the savior's glare
flashed falsely over the twelve
as they sat for the first time forming letters—
to your opposite, then, I turn:
though sleep still drags down
and the wheels' gargle spills me
with every other unready and contained
through the determined curve of fall, this is
one more hour that remains hers—
what has come back to itself from the four quarters
trembles, a needle that past nightfall has held
unveering though it went with me
and with you, her dark sister,
into the clean cold.

John Peck

"He who called blood builder..."

He who called blood builder is now memory, sound.
Dear, if we called blood wrecker we'd not lie,
but how thinly we should hear time's curved cutwater,
and never the full song of the falling pine,
that swish the nets make running through swells gone starry.

The steersman heard nothing, and then felt nothing,
toppling through the salt humus of passage.
And when Aeneas taking the tiller gathered
our woody landfall, the turning belt of worlds
spread out sparks of a brotherly burnishing.

Memory may work for us as did his mother
Venus, sluicing his wound invisibly,
its hurt going as a flood
                                    with which he heard
one life wash over and another rise,
but faster than remembering. He fought again,

and so the other thing may not be refused,
stand with me hearing it: from the bushy hill
the sound of fellings as huge nets hauled dripping,
plasma from slaughter clotting into nebular
founding stones, and smoke breathing screens of columns.

Zürich, the Stork Inn

Before you had been brought by the forceps beak
of the common tale, before we had been dropped
by the wide-winged forestaller
of questions, the quick question
of being born had been born
many times for the asking, yet still
waiting, Termia, for your mouth
to reframe it, for mine.

Set down beside the waters
of the Stork Inn, beneath
carousels and outsize
umbrellas, the spill of market Saturday—
leisurely miniature of what will win:
free play of forces setting
its own terms across all the stages...
stragglers caught by the throbbing or tinkly tune.
Whereas dark in your throat
gypsies huddled with cased violins
and zithers, cupped aside
from the tribes poured towards Sheol—
not harried this time, it was enough
that they played on your different keyboard.

And from the swung metal
of late summer towers, contradiction
of the anticipated and remembered,
belfries of a now,
camps and vast palaces of a sound
with no one center: from this
the ache to lift eyes wide
and hold them so, for whatever
might spring into beginning
though it fall short, through you, of the power to finish,
and helplessness, under the feathery surge
outward, to know which power may be more terrible.

Those you love you make stand
through a long vigil... so now
with the bonged bronze of ten towers concerted
through evening cloudburst
(Saint Alexander's day, though it is neither
his blood nor his forgotten life this fading
Zwinglian clangor seals)
and with snare drums of maskers
climbing towards a dragon
and gallows along a parapet,
I wait for the uptucked wings
of the ungainly bringer
to budge, for his unphrasable gift to cease

welling unpsalmed from afterbirth each instant,
for the prince of the powers of air,
earth, and underearth
to cease withholding homage from the mere seed…
thus watching one more hour,
while in the freshly wet
still tightening hemp of the noose
falls a body.

End of July

Of longing, Termia, the sharp specifics know
no end, and down its progress the sharp days
lose no edge, the hours
crumbling streambeds to strand
the source deeper in summer. Orchard ladders
lean into the moist sheen of dark globes.

Near Baden under swallows, one
belltower cut through vineyards, banners out,
when the wish fixed me, rash
as blind archery, to lift
one clean impulse streaking out of the ruck
even if it landed wide of your touch
while quarter-hour strokes
through worn maroon face rings rounded
on their gold mark.

Slow tones, swelling
things to a lightness—but if
that shivered me, it wasn't from forgetting
how separateness the cold angel converts us
to our fixities,
nor from denying she turns
each of us in her fire
like hickory seasoned for a torch,
nor from ceasing to share in her trade
of thrust, chill, thrust, the injustices

giving and taking justice in good time,
no one shouts the recognition,
it will not cry out in us,
yet they rang out, bronze
minutes, the bronze years,
with blunt frayed rope those changes
threading the spin of one swallow
who still climbed slabs of vapor thickening
over vine and crest, then
targeted down through harvest,
his poverty with ours
uncancelled yet his riches
plunging, sounding there
while counterweights
thudding inside their dry tower argued
you could not hear, and claimed no one could tell you
how they made medley, before the orisons
of Roman candles and rocket wails
broke from streets below:
Unification Eve.

Riposte

    No, don't ask us for
the heart as heart stood once,
don't expect...
        but I've heard
the bells of Cerveteri,
bells of Tarquinia, and
Fool, I said, *be quiet*,
neither dominion, prison,
nor single breaking of chains,
thus populous, these are
the bronze thymus of courage
and resignation, long interfering intervals—
no pope or Krupp to melt
their pulse, unchangeable—
while the folds of those tiles,

squares, tufted fields
roll out unharvestable,
irreparable, forage and wall
of seeming's harsh rumors,
of a held sound that hangs
out from us and colors
and claims the sometimes still
intolerable throb of body.

White Deer Running

Baucis and Philemon, having forgiven their killer Faust
and been resurrected to this life, to reenter their rest,
have come south and bought a stone house in the Morvan.
Undulating woodlots, hamlets beyond Autun.
Windows west only, into the long evenings
at midsummer, butterflies wavering in throngs
while rooms hold off heat with deep walls and embrasures.
Serendipity and sublimity are peasant sisters
waiting behind trees for farmers to find them, scuffle
with a pod of wild boar, and extend a barn from the wall.
Sublime and serendipitous, their last possession
for a renewed aging, lindens cooling each description.
The forest is named *Socrate*, a leader of the Resistance
dialectical in his disappearances,
and the barn was used for executions, by which side
there are varying reports. This too is to be had
in the idyll of ownership, a filmy disturbance
across the tabletop's oak grain, brown generations,
apples mounded in a plain crock, clear wines
draping colors over board and fruit, all this the senses
manufacturing from drift and ripple of syllables
before anything can be verified, yet the sheen falls
across an excellence of properties in trust
to no single appetite, in a place where sheen seems made fast.
	Narrow, the gate into our garden. A black sucking,
and waters crash, but you must not cry out or cling.

And then you are there, and you may come back if you choose
and report, though boasting is indecent, there are other ways.
Space there is not really different nor the sun,
but attachment is not what holds you, all that has gone.
         But that is
no possession: left listening and seeing, I was.
Apples, glass with ruddy window in its belly, the ruse
of solidity calling across the spoken was and is.
A low forest in Burgundy, woodlots in Massachusetts,
the last field before that drop where the river cuts.

     Against the clearing's edge
     at evening, already sliding
     among the indistinct
     stems of December trees,
     white deer running.
     It was perhaps an hour
     over the page, Arjuna's
     refusal and the protracted
     gleams of his charioteer.
     When I looked out the window,
     ranked birches turned in wind
     silver through shadow, over
     white deer standing.

Archaeus Terrae

rear ruth as the seat, rear her ureaus, cart cheer there
char the rat's tree, sear the cause, hate the rest
he, she errs, thee erreth, eaters at the heart
earth, aster, tar, hut, star are hers
use, re-use tears, her rarest chart
star's heat teases the archer's reach
thus true care, the scar, rehurts, reheats us
ear sure at the hatch, seer at such heat as
rush sheer arches through the scare—thereat, the rue, the hurt:
rust ate these earths at the heart's rate
at us, teacher, the art tears: steer us
each search reaches the harts there

Reichenau Afternoon

Here, hither, henceforth
                              the island's low arch
insinuates as would a self-easing breastbone
while the boat's diesels splutter.

A phrase in the broken, hieratic
rhythms of the beyond. Henceforth?
Where Strabo cleared weeds and hoed herbs
cataloguing them, ranging them in hexameters.

Spared, it may be, from awkward visions.
Speared like straight seed into plain labor
including his futile letters
to the brother kings.

Come, enter in with ass, oxen, the sudden
Kings and their gifts.
                          Under that memory
runs the deaf river, shifts in the bloody shores,
rearrangements of unsheltered ground.
But I am the island, lifted out how long
O Lord to hold into flows
reddened or sunned, and to breathe your starry
eclipses equally with the days
of your standing. I am island
and worker beneath its arches
and digger, shy of your wrath,
hoer to not go astray.

Woods Burial

At the rapids father and boy pitch in a young birch
    laid out by winter.

It is the March of mud roads and triggered hearts.
    That boy leaps as the limber corpse
    hurtles a chute, his father chuckles.

If they really knew what history is,
even though they're in it up to their necks,
they'd feel it, the tug, the cold tilt. They'd stand, shiver.

But how much smarter is that? And how am I better?
    It is that log I've got to be,
    shot straight, unstuck from the banks,
sluicing my wood–lice through the white gates,
        hurling home.

Getting at What Happens

There was a wife named Hope, who reconstructed every
stanza her husband, whizzed by the raven, could not inscribe.

Tarnish among tall gildings in the Hall of mirrors
sinks from infiltrating sun, parquetry crackles.

Sleek carter of first fire, Apollo from Louis's fountain,
aims horsepower at plate glass cooled before the revolutions.

Losses at hand, with lined faces, what have they
to do with the grassy palace, the dwindling and combed prospects?

Doctors pulled at the splinter
of fat in her Homeric heart, but she sang the days.

If one sways with it faithfully, the pendulum
takes back what it etched with dribbled sand. The sun also.

What they talked about in the cities, what they heard
their hearts fractioning, forecasting, was not all that happened.

A carpenter, planing and sanding,
stands and unstiffens, then hears them: mice in the rafters.

They talked about what they thought revolved inside them,
and what they thought had bitterly happened to them. And talked.

There was a wife named Luna, who had to reverse her tiara
whenever light filled it, annulling her fine entrance.

The old year, crone on the back of a Vézelay yeoman,
tends goose girls in the tale, her gift is love's beginning.

Joinery combs grainy solids, toothing them, to bend planes
seamlessly, then shut them fast. Where ends the beginning?

Ah but then blood happens, unstoppably, and so
why, then, a filmy stream of counter-gleams?

Room roofed over, stanza struck and ringing, meet in
the dancer's live arm, torsions of grazed pasture, forest.

Filthy hunters through them chase throat sound with horn sound,
hugged couples in the high grasses press closure to genesis.

Lancehead corroding there to dark bread, plow and tractor
tipping it forth, guards with damp sachet the queen's bedchamber.

And so the joints lock: sadness somewhere in it but finished,
its polish smells of hair and the gilded flooring of brooks.

And begins to press past even closeness, wing not the raven's
but hers who remembers, a mind past the hours, throbbing both ways.

Romanza

The untutored Richter showed us, but now there is this
bent girl. It is the middle of the long Andante.
The sufferer has penetrated her suffering,
not figuratively but really. One has to want to,
with the ancestors, and the race also, gathering.
She has convened them, the sign of which, hint to
radar watchers, is the shine of runoff trickling
form her hump. Its rock, concentrating into
quartzes, will show on their scanners as a searing
dot strengthening to core whiteness among scanty
blues repeating across sands of the swept ring.
She has found that part of Provence or Burgundy
in which honored ghosts abandoned a sunk dwelling,
and has poised herself on the chalk doorsill, twenty
horses champing within her thighs, and has cleared that rung
into, not space, not landscape, but their minty
lavendery cloud-mongering sandstone-levering
bed of forcings in the backmost band of mind, plenty
nor scarcity categories there, but emergence, ringing,
her elbows maintaining elevation while flinty
shoulders over wrists
                    from which everything
whatever its modes pours with cobalt coherence, chanty
or chorus. But there is no naming it now, only following.
She has found the chink, she has gotten through once
with the entire kit on her back, no slackening
of present actuality, its freight, and where that chance
has been taken it can be taken again, untrembling.
She has not protected herself with what the art wants
usually to shelter, nor has she done duty by fleeing
what the art in its deepening narrowness demands.
A sweaty cave has turned out into heart's shattering.
Gone landforms into future beachheads, the homelands.
Future? The rarely present, the abiding there unfolding.

Incident near Vicenza

Bright, yes, but this is the floor of the crypt,
where Adam was told to scratch a groove with his foot
when cloud printed it—

though you would have me lose
even that bare grasp of my law
and the law of heat-shimmer over rock, Termia,
though you meant to veil
every rupture, you cannot bar
my stumbling fall towards the unpredicted
sanctum, its explosion
in furnaces of the dust.

           And so
it was not worth your while trying to stop
the hill road from sliding under
or the crest from descending and leveling out:
behind me you were not,
nor before,
         and through my plodding
it wasn't worth tallying
the count that your heartbeat's mimicry
pad-padded in sliding shadow's
meeting of each downstroke
on earth, sweetish solar
talcum and the angels'
improbable residue—
in them there, sounding! Your rhythm, meetingless
greeter, boundaryless mapper, counterfeited
the burden of appointments
missed and never to be made, and canceled
relief where mass grew mighty
at last: from far, from within,
from every side to the one point
declared past all law by geometers
of the furious inch and spearing
light-year, it was neither of us

who took on substance there,
but rather that which everywhere stands, fleshless fire
able to score its own sign, its gash
of crushed squirrel in the rut
beneath three swooning lupines, and below them
a severed mountain's gleaming
quarry of chalk.

Trio Threaded on Lines from the Parthian Hymns

Grasp happiness with this leavetaking!

Wet strew from sycamores
shot my boot out towards the bend of Tiber
    when I was halfway down
stone risers to the embankment's mulled gibber,

    quietest lappings, and toss
of trash, rufflings of dusk-muffled gulls,
    like muted strings for the stripes
squiggled from lamps down the depth's sliding pulls,

    all this registering
in the swift tilt of the world away, rolled gap,
    as my head sought its hard pillow
and my frame slithered through that stair's loose grip.

    How much quieter there:
overhead, on all sides, the withdrawn traffic.
    Farther, the slide of dark cloud.
Dank smells, no annals, no lights. Cold flow prolific.

    Long before I learned
that Pasolini dropped to the same view here,
    stunned, I looked up at it,
two meters thin, history's glitter and fear.

Buonarotti's bridge,
Cocles's clicking sword, the litter of bills
    from American cars on the night
of the elections; up there, on the seven hills.

    As in a kiva's hub
a gully lets the dancer burrow down
    under a trap and fling it
flagrantly back and shoot out as god, clown,

    and with his anomaly
focus the plane he returns to, so, with fury,
    jackanapes, go on up,
with innocence the blow has restored, go, harry!

        you were jailed in the roaring void
        and dragged captive over every threshold.

Into dens of approbation
    in the dun north
was ushered the anomalous
disturber and refiner, desolation's
allegorist who drove forth
from his south the ripe figures, scandalous—

vitalities as victims, throttled
    or trumped, or married
whitely to mortuary meats,
himself the stainer of youth, fabled mottled
stingwing to the staid virtues, ferried
for brief honoraria to the sweet seats.

The villa with dusky screening room.
    To the book signing.
The watering hole of the prize-givers.
To the seminar. Assiduously bright gloom.
He entertained their questions. Dining
quickly, he abandoned them, the long livers,

he enplaned once again for hell,
    and entered standing,

ambassador of the pierced boys,
of men who although sold out would not sell
something of a countermanding
fantasy, nourished against increasing noise,

and stupor of empty liberties,
    and garbage stenches
in their own streets, and the tiredness
everywhere, most at the heart of hot energies,
most even in the loins and haunches
of consolation, wearied out to weirdness.

And there a few of the servitors
    bashed in his skull
and shattered his hand and ruptured his heart with the wheels
of his own car, where Tiber snores
out to vastness, where the legendary null
of Hades began once, and bright mist steals.

> *you orbited through the whirl of births,*
> *you were pillaged in all the cities.*

    Pastorals have flown
out with the probe, or in, down the cell's helix.
    Zero trajectory,
or else picnickers in the Mendelian calyx.

Between, I stretch a giddy cable.
    Towards you I balance,
Persephonèia, you said you'd return,
and so my left hand I shall let wobble
as reason, my right as dalliance,
between the infinities a rhythm to learn.

Flown and dissolved, while the rampart spreads.
    Perhaps a neglected
fountain burbles yet in the garden,
the weedy center. But certainly the dead
shall live, out on the unprotected
wind sag of the wire, where you hum them pardon.

John Peck

"Giovanni…"

Giovanni, would you
see me
alle cinque, Chiesa Nuova?
To talk, I have to.

Overworked teacher
and weary
paterfamilias,
shy would-be searcher…
we had been guests
at a friend's.
Now I sat where the Corso
Vittorio thrusts

widest, the smooth
steps ripple
away from the barney church
and pigeons breathe

stertorously
among bronze
hours, and watched a protest
march gather hoarsely

in the oblong square,
the blind
gypped by the state led there
by the blind to roar
through their bull horns
and step off
in waveringly good order.
    A cart of melons

got sideswiped by
a leathery
motorcyclist, who doffed
helmet and drew

up to the splatter
and paid for
three more than he had smashed.
The old man twittered.

A waif on crutches
swung and
swung through the mess with whoops
kicking swatches
of rind, a crone
cackling
back of him filched one up
to taste, alone...

Then it was those
I'd remarked
other evenings, now brushing
strangers, and haze
from the late rush
acridly
holding the heat, and the whole
air of it threshing
slowly and greatly
up through
that vast parlor, none of us
explicitly
invited, over
our criss-cross
making for the blue ceiling
with a sound never

quite spoken out
and a fragrance
obscurely of the occasion,
of all those there met—

    so I sat for
three hours,
and the desperate man never showed,
who in his rare

delicacy
had dispatched
all that company, all
those beings to me—
their half or no greeting,
or straight on,
aiming at something we all sensed,
moving, or waiting—

my appointment
was with them,
and now, these years since, with
this deep content.

Barn Doorway in July

Where may heart open through the lockstep of evil and good?
Weathered doors divide along a rail on dot wheels.
Blurred, the hankering after harvests. No one stands there,
while midway a shaggy sphere of petals, and bees stirring
geranium eternity, weave scent and low sound.
Faint essence that quilts the commander-in-chief's guilt
as he treads the red weave to his bath, sealord sacrificer,
and quilts too Lulu's shriek, cradling wrath and frail form
while the hum thrusts melody for her first seed—
this hangs by chain, flows from a tub of garden pinks
dealt through chalky whites: commonest companions
hosting hummingbird now and a star's heat, those
interlacing frequencies wrap-thronged and arrowed.
Contemplation is the wing, sang the Victorine.
Here it whirrs to feed on light, its other self.
Ever from two, all the rest. From that, a portal.
And then darkness, musty generations of grass ghosts,
swayed spines of milk's bearers twitching off flies.
Captain, courtesan, those stained excellences,
                                          go through.
Why have all other eyes watched them if not for this.

When I thought I had missed destiny, these
gathered and passed, startling pair though inevitable.
No bridge from death in the bad to death in the good, declareth
the whole, ant's mandible nibbling what the shark dribbled,
yet that couple strode over into forgiveness and vanished.
When it is too much, and when it is never enough, the doors
have been, already, drawn open over this cooling cave.
Across the unblazed trail with the trodden, the threadbare with the fresh.
And if that is so long since, I must have witnessed it.
Though blank here, I am in the knowledge. And souls, the bees.

Unfinished Announcement

A deep cough hauls me up and heaves me
into the third night of clear phlegm.

Into the small hours the lamp of the world out.
My bedroom a freighter's crow's nest over barely felt engines.

The changes are coming in, they require
this slowness over dark water.

The maple close by the window needs to extend every nerve
out over an Atlantic sliding like slate beneath it.

In my book still open, a young widower at night has glimpsed
his dead wife in a London blank as a fogged dockyard.

She also stares at him. And slowly they *know*. The whole real deep of it.

She still feels life, life of a kind, carrying her,
muting, absorbing, yet entering the same and leaving the same,

although she knows that change has overtaken her.
The changes need to push through each cell.

The prow needs to hold itself unrustable and gleaming
even down and black, into endless water.

What does a blackbird see, clamped twiggy over the sliding wet slabs?

After the spasms, in lamplight the same yet newly absorbent,
a question newly spreads, I cannot see out of it—

is this strange sameness the great alteration, death's afterward?
Even through the fingers extends difference.

Breathing too differs though it resumes above the slow rushing.
An impulse to leap and bang things, even that dampens.

The test lies in the odd clarity stretching out past finger ends.
Renewal, what everyone has asked for: it extends here.

But this time there are to be no ceremonies.
When morning comes the miracle will go in everywhere.

Dimensions into the photograph, the next red into the painting.
Coming from our houses we shall blink.

Not giving any sign, but full of the knowledge.
For he saw her truly. And seeing him she had been certain.

Coming from our doorways into day, we shall
dispense with any reservations.

Each man, each woman, will carry the opening after shutting it
and be that framelessness. But not dance, not shout.

For only the whole unfolding will let us get the sense of it down,
the entire day, and the night, and the oncoming ocean of night-day.

The swift low swell riding through tamped granulars.
Met eyes vanishing. Unlocking hands filled. Earth, released wave.

Passage

Under the seen, neither lap nor long embrace,
it is like the progress by canal barge out of Dijon
past the lockmasters' houses, and it is like those houses,
each a cottage with geraniums but in squared granite,
fitted out with brass numerals and a hand semaphore
so that through sunny hours the apparition of domestic
singularity and solidity gets stamped with the impress
of Dutch replication, bureaucratic weight, military snap.
But a snap drifting into porosity, dusted with somnolence
of alerts met routinely and the heavy swish of watergates.
On ahead, the arc of an angler's rod under plane trees
just where the flatness, beginning to bend, deceptively
takes its hazed mirrorings and gnat swirls through zero aperture.
It is like the suspension, neither glide nor plunge,
that makes of thick red paint along the ferruled moldings
and tubular handrails a proposition to be decoded
by one of the philosophers of layers, rabbis of baklava.
There is the truth beyond
                        question, unquestionably.
Passage, beyond beginning or beginning again,
is its portal, and likeness in passing keeps it open.
Likeness a sunned moth on that handrail: my friend's hand,
and passing is like air in the shore grass after wind,
moisture and scent among the growth on that arm, also
like breath at its cusps, intake or outflow, in the throat's column
unspeaking, hunting no pitch, anticipating no thought.
Motion pressed off bow and sucked off rudder as one swirl.
Like, like; it is like a simile, a comparison stepping off
one stone because it has found another in the amber pour.
Not simply steering down a channel, this voyage. And the thrush begins.

Violin

With all pasts and futures harboring in this present
then all, happiness and unhappiness, is a choice
if only because I have agreed to build here. Yet even
the most daring choose happiness alone, and thinking
will never get me through this, and feeling loiters in it—
only Great Harbor floats all of it, trembly, waiting.
Following descriptions of the North Pyramid at Dashur,
the Red Pyramid stripped of its red sandstone facing,
then photographs from recent expedition reports,
I found no speculations about precisely why
this pivotal structure slopes at forty-three degrees,
a matter of moment, perhaps or perhaps not, yet
I saw sand shelving along the base of the west face,
a ripply ledge smoothing along remnant facing
and blending with it—the same as on Plum Island,
barrier beach for piping plover and pale-belled sand shrubs
dropping its steep bevel sucked at for miles by surf,
the rolling sound momently sinking away in it,
its high edge fronting dune grass nervy against sun.
No Joseph among us to build granaries, no Jonah
to ironize destruction, no Jacob to hammer choice.
One third through the mere sixty years that saw the great
pyramids rise, this one, with the lowest inclination
at forty-three degrees, *cautious* some say to forestall
shiftings that skewed the vitals of the Bent Pyramid
somewhat earlier and three quarters of a mile off,
was the first achieved prototype. A slope that has me sense
greater mass and area than it commands. A discovery
about proportion and it may be an application
of lore no one yet has been able to read from the record.
This time the architect lifted the burial chamber
higher inside the mass—the squared cone of sunlight—
and for the first time aligned the coffin east-west
with tomb temple and the sun's track. Its capstone
pyramidion was of the same red sandstone,
not the gilded white stone or granite of later practice.
The entire casing bulged slightly outward much like

the faint entasis on a Greek column, though not
meant for Greek good looks, but rather for what would stand.
Altering the slope's angle rise by rise with
cord and peg, masons jesting with the overseer:
this innovation in masonry was not imitated.
Senefru, who enjoyed people, calling his staff *Dear Friend*,
the only king known for doing so, presided over
erection of the Bent and the Red pyramids, as well as
two others at Meidum and Seila, the start on Egypt's
Manhattan Project, four solar fusion battery casings
for his charged body, at three locations. He was buried
in this one if its hurried completion is any evidence.
Osiris's theology by then nosed ahead of the astral one.
An east–west journey at night with the sun in that god's boat.
Setting out through river reeds, their silken forgivingness.
On one side, barrier dunes thrusting up into solar acetylene
which tracks with me along their apex, while on the other
vast drenchings sink into the low slope. Four fiberglass
fishing poles shoot lines off into surf, their necks
bent studiously, their shanks in tubes rammed into sand,
their armchair owner dozing under a blue towel.
Four nylon zings of tackle as if sounding unison.
They baked loaves for him in the reliefs. He himself ran
a race in the Heb–Sed ceremony, as did his fathers,
all in renewal of their powers, his predecessor loping
hugely across the slab that seals a shaft at Meidum.
Though no tides any longer moisten the stones, those tunnels
smell of the sea. The burial of full-scale ships
began under his son Khufu near the vast piles at Giza.
My ears ring with a cricket-like susurrus that comes from years
of holding taut line out into the oncoming rush.
A certain age renders further ambition supernumerary,
my buried boats need no more cult. For all the forces
at play in this wide theater, its spaciousness declares
a propertyless state. May I now take up
the violin that nearly came to me at age ten,
my maternal uncle's gift? Brought ceremoniously
on a special visit, yet it went back with him, the fact of it
raising an outsize grief in my mother for herself, perhaps.
Rest in peace and the mystery, with the silent thing in its case.

Or may I pursue this engineering further?—surrogate
for the womanly body of that fiddle gone downstream.
Yet they were building spirit reservoirs, surge tanks
for seam voltage, soul-welding solar granaries, and one architect
had been chief priest. The hand tracking shadow at Dashur
from rod to rod for the foundation's first course of stones
may have held a lamp for priests in the last chamber
as rare privilege—for their ordained invocations
tested by many sequencings, happiness on alert
through ordeals, the chances awful and the aim real.
I woke with the sand grains of his destiny alive
across my maroon blanket, mustard golden spores
thrown over him by the king, a gift of land to that
Dear Friend. Deir of the geometries. His eye through the pile,
its red slope, the Forty-Three: design stabilizes the *mana*
of earth lofted into fire's force and held there,
steadies the dangerous changes. Guards against them
even before the end, so that a fine instrument
recharged and tuned during the royal run but at last
taken away may morph to mastery in some other walk
by another sea. May turn—mangled god—mischance into the path.
For this I sing: Deir of the triangle with plumb line
portable and pendulous in his eye's mind intending
this for the powers, the king and people, the realms
interlocking, past calamities, through dynasties dangling
in the shaky cycles of order.
                              I took from his case the still shiny
stream-bottom varnish of the thing and chin-clasped it
per his instruction, and before setting it back in the inky
blue plush drew one long wavery whine
from the G string, pushing up slowly with the bow.
Delight broke from his face. The dark closure not yet
having come across hers, she parted her lips, eyebrows
arching expectantly. Labored, nursed, caressed, that sound
could go on past the end of its own curve, such was
its Pythagorean hint even in my raw hand,
animal miracle among the ratios.
Next morning it was gone. This then sing:
that were I to walk that sand's bandwidth between desert
and facing stone, I would tread neither the waste

nor the monument, but one string stretched like the dune's world
behind my barrier beach, scrub and wiry foliage
nestled minutely into pockets of the in-between
and giving ear steadfastly to immensity.
That close to forty-three degrees is where the G string
lands a bow's tilt, as a pro will testify.
That even the smudge across her happiness, and the murderous
touch of *creatura*, and the inept weight of fate,
dissolve where the soul burns and melts, where tone
and overtone release each other, and if all stabilized things vanish
in the furnace, truing the line and lighting the chant
give love to the fire. An immense fragrance rose
from the dyed velvet of the case, the sealed wood,
strings, rosin, fogged bakelite of the chin cup,
the untreated inner wood of the curved body,
the equine substance of the glue, the fluted pegs,
ivory nut to tauten the pale sheaf of horsetail,
and a man's sweat and breath, when he opened these to me.
I have not imagined myself long in the burial chamber,
neither as carver nor priest, and only for a brief spell as builder
scanning the ceiling slab for telltale cracks. A vast
aroma lifted from that case among the bright faces.

Book of the Dead? We Have no Book of the Dead

*I have done no evil... I have not caused pain... I have caused no weeping... I have not
brought suffering to anyone... I have not copulated, I have not misbehaved.*

Not that powers themselves fade. Their grip on us lessens.
The final Apollo has been caulked and polished, the last
Aphrodite sanded, oiled, and catalogued. It is time.
Unrolling it down the pasture like a banquet tablecloth,
helpers to the balloonist spread his red means
slashed with puce and white like the puffed thighs of Swiss
halbardiers at the Vatican, then they holler.
Igniting the latent core of actuality,
torching the anthropomorphism that passes for it,
he aims a tubular frame into the vast yoke.

Billows undulate around its bass hissing and swell.
In a mauve frock coat from his great-grandfather's day,
even though he is a sifter of fissionables
in the era of miasmas, he pats a grey top hat, silver buttons.
Pats his waist-high son, and checks the wicker pannier.
His appearance says, *No I am not capable of this.*
No, I have nothing to do with any of it,
no, not this technē. Yet he will sail jetting flame
in momentary dragonings up through puffed pleats.
It has begun already: they stirruped him into the basket
and slackened the anchoring guy ropes. The schools
of philosophy were once ardent gangs competitive
about the task: how to live. Caps wave, hankies.
They worked out the protocols, tensed the cords, slipped them,
the separation they celebrate gives a master to freedom.
Such nuptials of possibility with discipline
rely on a harmonic of tricks. Usually the flame
wobbles, destroying. Gilda Larocca, taken in Florence
in 'forty-four while running the short-wave, escaped to Milan
with retinas scorched by the torturer's lights. She had said,
No, I didn't know that. No. No. She could still type,
and so two patents, for ink that lovers could daub on rose petals
and a couch that became a coffin, passed through her machine.
A weightless stationery for amor in hell's hour
and a seat you take with you into weightlessness: the *No*
begins to slide onto wilting surfaces.
For Old Top Hat, the basket stays basket. His frock coat
is no mesmeric bon-bon of the escape artist.
His drift is not away, but across the live and furry
in a mirror of the dive. He wagers the dimensions,
up as down, as free-fall, and pollen big as towns,
a seeing particle among the particles, roar then silence.
Metaphysician, and how not watch him? Craning my neck back,
again I see boys drop snowballs down the face of Strasbourg's
cathedral, who, if interrogated would say, *No we didn't do that,*
while what attacked was not their toys, it was the air:
a stinging tartness with molecular teeth, supplements
from Trinity, the Reich, Poland, Japan, Brazil, Bikini
through one lifespan. Whiteness muffled the whole cliff
though one might still hear, in all the languages, *No, we didn't,*

no, not us. Couples at the portal under the gallery
gawked up at dots enlarging then ducked among the layered saints and queens.
And here I am watching a maestro:
he leans from the rim coiling in a rope, receding
as slowly as Mr. Tanimoto in Hiroshima's park
rowing his loads away from the flames with a bamboo pole.
The fire works for him this time. They are safe. He is diving.
Through his ropes the buzz of the lived plane resolves to a hum,
pattern and heaviness apart for an interval.
From the third outrider of an unnumbered sun, lifting
as diving—this, too, the human may arrange and patent
if it has sat to its task, lived its dual nature,
for though sandbag conscience will lift with it, grey ballast,
all has been readied by sandy Egyptian sagacity
to deny complicity. For it is human to say,
No, I have never sinned, no, not, bare-faced to the powers.

Random-bench

When we bought round-trip tickets from Brig
to the high valley town *Rundfahrt für zwei*
our main aim was the curving climb
and the corridor window up to let us put our heads out
like children against orders, the leaning red coaches squealing
against the arcing rails.
We had not studied the schedule: the only time
you did not carry the timetable in your head
as cleanly as the declensions you still knew
twenty years downstream from Pindar and his Chiron.
At the end of the line we went straight for the turret
of the stone-roofed chapel,
finally opening the little blue book:
there were three minutes until the next train
(which of course was the same train).
The conductor laughed, *Why not stay at least for a coffee!*
Staying wasn't the point, we said, it was the getting-there,
disciples of Browning or Rashid al-Din

the world historian who never ceased his time travel
although he sat quite still.
We hang out the same window now on the other side
up-alley through firs and bouldery cuts and steep pasture.
The toy coach is half-empty, our seat
a matte green vinyl in the second-class compartment
abandoned, free in sun through rain-stain over the glass.
I turn once to look at it, the sun sitting there green and quite still.
More and more that practice makes sense:
the other fellow who is with me at all times
is claiming more of his due.
Silently insists on acknowledgment.
Asserts his seniority with Nuremburg but also with slow breathing.
Since you are elsewhere
I cannot ask if I told you about the two Pindar scholars .
one in his hotel room on the Isle de la Cité
and the other coming in from the suburbs on the crowded local to meet him.
The meeting was my idea. I told the owner
at her desk in the tiny lobby, a woman of probity,
to ring us in the first man's room when the second one asked for us.
We waited an hour, chatting over white wine, cheese.
Number two is rocking one leg over the other in that lobby
on the settee there, silk-cushioned.
The owner has told him that we will be down presently.
She has just put down the telephone for the fourth time.
Yet she never called us—we tested the connection
after Pindar Two left angrily
and Pindar One went with me to investigate, too late.
Pindar Two is on the local back out of the Gard du Nord,
the drab facades of the flats shining and peeling from his lenses.
The late-afternoon debate that would have oiled
the very hinge of process,
the precedence of wind or rain—which?—in their long partnership
and whether the rest of existing Greek poetry supports Pindar's
placement of rain first, still hangs over the settee,
silky stripey abandoned maroon and butterscotch.
In suburbs back from the main line
Tsvetaeva reworked love letters
to her Berlin publisher who had cooled toward her,
planing them into French, urgent to print a small book in Paris,

retooling his left hand to lift and smother it in the new vocabulary,
violet-brown Borscht jelling on her stove
when I was so close to you on that random-bench
pour longtemps—très longtemps…
cette banquette au hazard,
cette banquette abandonée.
The meetings depend on precision.
At your corner desk by the window you sit through the morning
turning German entries on Greek myths into handbook English
then straightening in a spasm: *Incest and murder!*
Fratricide, matricide, parricide, murder and incest!
And no telling which came first.
The work is there for us both, badly paid though constant.
The walk we take between spells of it high into the Grisons
with picnic lunch to the cobalt lake
has us turn back as soon as we get there
because our hostess had clocked the route and cautioned us.
In fact she hurries toward us on the road from her house,
Russia has fallen! It is too late to alert the telegrapher
on the express taking Tsvetaeva back there for her son's sake
true to her rebuke
of poets who went with history instead of against it.
The great Islamic historian of the world
shifts his bony arse on his chair cushion, and one more khan
stands installed at court. They sliced Rashid's Jewish head off
a decade after Dante fled Florence. Came the wind.
The meetings are where all the real living is, says Buber
looking up from his timetable and clicking the ticket-punch
six times in rapid succession.
I see that your keenness with schedules and grammar
although steadily going with us those years
also occupied a cubby in first-class,
no one else seated there, the sun blue on its plush
instead of the matte green vinyl.
It steeps and warms over the roar.
Came the rain though the two Pindars never had it out,
whether rain running before the wind
or rain lipping and smothering the wind's hand
only the waiting sun on the settee knows.
Convoking both the dead in under-earth and the ever-living in sky

around the spindle of his chanted performance,
Ur–Pindar both waited and moved. And cried out.
And galvanized benches in smooth half rings before the dancing circle.
Someone invaluable and dearly vexing
was here just now and is not.
And now the birth-rates fall both in Detroit and Seattle
as they did for the Soviets before their collapse.
There is peace in the solid hot pour
back from the window's gusts
onto the green seat that waits for you
before your blown hair pulls back in and resettles,
Chiron's mane agile, mortal,
immortal teacher of the heroes.

Dawn Renga

El aire de la almena
San Juan de la Cruz

Mist from the mountain
unraveling, or is it
the mountain that tears

    Where lightning scattered the loons
    river steams up into day

He of the Cross, hid
in his bright darkness, lay
stroking wind-washed hair

    Under the fan of cedars
    when the Lover struck his neck

He mentioned also
a battlement, the wind there,
but no place was safe

Beheaded with all others
who suffered through to union

Hold the affliction
given, perceived by no one,
until you can see

all the rock ledges at once,
all the climbers, swift seasons

and it is the earth
growing suddenly before
a broad sky crumbling

earth headless and giving birth
to itself, warm wind steady

Let me title these notes "Sight-Line 2008," for several poems selected here attend to the same premonitory mood that I have worked through in a near majority of my writing. Far from being alone in sensing a blind rush toward nemesis, none the less I have sensed something like it from earliest memory. There is nothing special about that fact, since it stems from both my nature and early conditioning, in ways that are shared with any number of people. It also seconds a motion made perennially in writing's long parliament. In the largest view, one might say that as phylogenetic layers of the mind quicken, a radio's crystal set crackles, or that as the pterodactyl's wing crooks an angel lifts off.

In longer forms not sampled here ("March Elegies," "A Gross of Poems in the Mixed Manner," "From the Gardens of Copenhagen," "Round," "M," and "San Andrean" One and Two), the same mood has been at work. Melville called these prospects "loomings." Every great-great-grandnephew of Baudelaire knows them, rag-pickers fishing up the known with the unknown or the finished with the raw. And one cannot set out to do this; it happens.

Two lines from an early poem, "Cider and Vesalius," anticipate these matters by inscribing a tightly gnarled version of them. "The eye / Burs, rinsing her blind hives…" That clause identifies the queen bee, sole orienteer for the swarm when her hive relocates. The eye there does not *blur*, as one might expect, but instead sharply provokes its own tears, flushing out the old way of doing things and thereby somewhat anticipating the queen's role. Unwittingly in these lines I set myself a koan about the mood that I am scoping here. I still remember the correction that intervened as I was about to inscribe the customary verb *blurs*. Only the compact symbolic act would do, the left hand insisted: use the odd verb that half-voices the expected one.

That particular turn risks a bit of darkness, in the way of overload rather than through the several modern and postmodern styles of irony. It sacrifices momentary clarity to an earnest wager.

Of course, "sacrifice" is a loaded word for writing that does not come from taking a definite stand at personal cost to the writer. Yet it still identifies a common task, that of bearing up through one's complicity and ignorance in a dominant mass society through the long twentieth century. That is, the individual counts for more than the system in only one way. Only the single person can choose to assume the burden of change, which the mass by its nature cannot choose to do. In this way one's fellows can be eased of that much of the load. Neither a moral exemplar nor a prophet, the poet at least puts ear to the rails of that sacrificial responsibility. Oscar Milosz, a genuinely prophetic writer, addressed the inner sound of his own intuition as something both true to unfolding event yet also "traveling farther than time," echo-laden yet also eerily ahead of the game.[1]

Among the selections here, "Hazelnut" scans the kind of intuition that I would call my own as a hologramic, total shape. "Barn Doorway in July" likewise treats it as "the whole." Other poems render it as fluid transits between past and future: "Leaving the Central Station," "Zürich, the Stork Inn," "Riposte," and "Getting at What Happens." No philosopher lurks behind these configurations. One is more primitive, like a fish. The dream of the Arab in Book V of Wordsworth's *The Prelude* forebodes no particular end of the world. The flood loosed in Yeats's "The Second Coming," written in 1921, does not predict the cataclysm that renewed itself in 1939. ("Mere anarchy" is massive, indiscriminate, and tidal, through Yeats's bilingual pun on "*mer.*") For all the taxonomic assurances given to us that the Romantic and modernist eras have ended, neither of these two letters from Wordsworth and Yeats has yet arrived at its destination. Between the world as Simone Weil's obdurately closed door, and the world as Blake's precociously modern realm of hyperspaces, lies the tension field of the *creatio continua*. The heroic age of psychology has made these matters no less real to writers, but it has taught them to foreswear metaphysical naivety about the place occupied by that same field. Therefore I invoke the primitive again: without pretending to know the meaning of whatever is being ducked, one may still perceive meaning *qua* feeling,

1 My translation of "Le roi Don luis..." in *The Noble Traveler: The Life and Writings of O.V. de L. Milosz*, ed. Christopher Bamford, intro. Czesław Miłosz (West Stockbridge MA: Lindisfarne Press, 1985), pp. 86–7.

consciously entertaining emotion's compact signals, two-way affairs fore-connected in the backward and abysm of switchgear. Such is the territory.

Robert Archambeau has singled out "Woods Burial" in *M and Other Poems* (1996) as the point at which I raised the bar for myself, making what had earlier been material into the occasion for a task. In other words, he saw that I was ready to step around or through the given mood of anticipation. Several of the poems here, which follow that book, make a bid to meet his challenge.

For the most part the selections appear chronologically. Five are uncollected: "*Giovanni,*" "Book of the Dead? We Have no Book of the Dead," "Violin," "*Random-bench,*" and "Dawn Renga," the last in fact preceding "Violin" on the calendar but here providing a round-off. Poet Rudolph Borchardt was the twentieth-century translator of Virgil, Pindar, and Dante into German. "Zürich, the Stork Inn" borrows a title from Paul Celan (his poem commemorates a postwar meeting there with Nelly Sachs). "Interleaved Lines..." (p. 134) experimentally writes consecutive reflections with right and left hands, one set to the left margin and the other indented. "Archaeus Terrae" (p. 143) treats a key phrase from Paracelsus to anagramatic play. In "Getting at What Happens" (p. 145) the woman named Hope (in Russian, Nadezhda) doubles for Osip Mandelshtam's widow. Her husband is the unnamed figure in "He who called blood builder."

John Peck

ROBERT PINSKY

Robert Pinsky's poetry collection *Gulf Music* was published in 2007. His earlier works include *The Figured Wheel* (1996), awarded the Lenore Marshall Prize and *The Inferno of Dante* (1994), which won the Howard Morton Landon Prize for translation and the *Los Angeles Times* Book Award. His prose works include *The Life of David* (2005), an account of the Biblical hero. A three-time Poet Laureate of the United States, Pinsky founded the Favorite Poem Project; the project's most recent anthology is *An Invitation to Poetry* which includes a DVD featuring Americans reading and talking about beloved poems. His works about poetry include *The Sounds of Poetry* (1998) and *Democracy, Culture and the Voice of Poetry* (2002), based on his Tanner Lectures on Human Values, given at Princeton University. Pinsky is the poetry editor of the online magazine *Slate* and teaches in the graduate creative writing program at Boston University.

Book

Its leaves flutter, they thrive or wither, its outspread
Signatures like wings open to form the gutter.

The pages riffling brush my fingertips with their edges:
Whispering, erotic touch this hand knows from ages back.

What progress we have made, they are burning my books, not
Me, as once they would have done, said Freud in 1933.

A little later, the laugh was on him, on the Jews,
On his sisters. O people of the book, wanderers, *anderes*.

When we've wandered all our ways, said Ralegh, Time shuts up
The story of our days—Ralegh beheaded, his life like a book.

The sound *bk*: lips then palate, outward plosive to interior stop.
Bk, bch: the beech tree, pale wood incised with Germanic runes.

Enchanted wood. Glyphs and characters between boards.
The reader's dread of finishing a book, that loss of a world,

And also the reader's dread of beginning a book, becoming
Hostage to a new world, to some spirit or spirits unknown.

Look! What thy mind cannot contain you can commit
To these waste blanks. The jacket ripped, the spine cracked,

Still it arouses me, torn crippled god like Loki the schemer
As the book of Lancelot aroused Paolo and Francesca

Who cling together even in Hell, O passionate, so we read.
Love that turns or torments or comforts me, love of the need

Of love, need for need, columns of characters that sting
Sometimes deeper than any music or movie or picture,

Robert Pinsky

Deeper sometimes even than a body touching another.
And the passion to make a book—passion of the writer

Smelling glue and ink, sensuous. The writer's dread of making
Another tombstone, my marker orderly in its place in the stacks.

Or to infiltrate and inhabit another soul, as a splinter of spirit
Pressed between pages like a wildflower, odorless, brittle.

Antique

I drowned in the fire of having you, I burned
In the river of not having you, we lived
Together for hours in a house of a thousand rooms
And we were parted for a thousand years.
Ten minutes ago we raised our children who cover
The earth and have forgotten that we existed.
It was not maya, it was not a ladder to perfection,
It was this cold sunlight falling on this warm earth.

When I turned you went to Hell. When your ship
Fled the battle I followed you and lost the world
Without regret but with stormy recriminations.
Someday far down that corridor of horror the future
Someone who buys this picture of you for the frame
At a stall in a dwindled city will study your face
And decide to harbor it for a little while longer
From the waters of anonymity, the acids of breath.

The Thicket

The winter they abandoned Long Point Village—
A dozen two-room houses of pine frames clad
With cedar faded to silver and, not much whiter
Or larger, the one-room church—they hauled it all
Down to the docks on sledges, and at high tide
Boats towed the houses as hulks across the harbor
To set them on the streets of Provincetown.
Today they're identified by blue tile plaques.
Forgotten the fruitless village, in broken wholes
Transported by a mad Yankee frugality
Sweating resolve that pickled the sea-black timbers.

The loathsome part of American Zen for me
Is in the Parable of the Raft: a traveler
Hacks it from driftwood tugged from the very current
That wedged it into the mud, and lashes it
With bitter roots he strips between his teeth.
And after the raft has carried him across
The torrent in his path, the teacher says,
The traveler doesn't lift the raft on his back
And lug it with him on his journey: oh no,
He leaves it there behind him, doesn't he?
There must be something spoiled in the translation—

Surely those old original warriors
And ruling-class officials and Shinto saints
Knew a forgetting heavier than that:
The timbers plunged in oblivion, hardened by salt;
Black, obdurate throne-shaped clump of ancient cane-spikes
At the raspberry thicket's heart; the immigrant
Vow not to carry humiliations of the old
Country to the new, but still infusing the segmented
Ingested berry encasing the seed, the scribble
Of red allegiances raked along your wrist;
Under it all, the dead thorns sharper than the green.

Veni, Creator Spiritus

Blessed is He who came to Earth as a Bull
And ravished our virgin mother and ran with her
Astride his back across the plains and mountains
Of the whole world. And when He came to Ocean,
He swam across with our mother on his back.
And in His wake the peoples of the world
Sailed trafficking in salt, oil, slaves and opal.
Hallowed be His name, who blesses the nations:
From the Middle Kingdom, gunpowder and Confucius.
From Europe, Dante and the Middle Passage.
Shiva is His lieutenant, and by His commandment
Odysseus brought the palm tree to California,
Tea to the Britons, opium to the Cantonese.
Horses, tobacco, tomatoes and gonorrhea
Coursed by His will between Old Worlds and New.
In the Old Market where children once were sold,
Pirated music and movies in every tongue,
Defying borders as Algebra trans-migrated
From Babylon to Egypt. At His beck
Empire gathers, diffuses, and in time disperses
Into the smoky Romance of its name.
And after the great defeat in Sicily
When thousands of Athenians were butchered
Down in the terrible quarries, and many were bound
And branded on the face with a horse's head,
Meaning *this man is a slave*, a few were spared
Because they could recite new choruses
By the tragedian Euripides, whose works
And fame had reached to Sicily—as willed
By the Holy One who loves blood sacrifice
And burnt offerings, commerce and the Arts.

In Defense of Allusion

The world is allusive. The mantis alludes to a twig
To deflect the starling, the starling is a little stare
Alluded to by Shakespeare: Jacques-Pierre,

His name alluding not to spears or beers
Or shaking, though the mantis does tremble a little,
Helpless refugee. Or I imagine she does,

Feeding that fantasy to my heart, an organ
Alluded to by the expression "courage"
Like "Shakespeare" from the French, *M.* Jack-Peter.

They say his father was a secret Catholic,
The sort of thing that could get a person killed.
Religion is nearly always a terrible thing

And even allusion sometimes is full of harm—
Though it means *play*—as when the President promised
To defeat terrorism with a great crusade.

His writers doubtless didn't mean to allude
To the Christians, including Richard *Coeur de Lion*
And several bishops, who made Jerusalem's gutters

Run bloody not as an image or figure of speech.
Lion-Heart nestled in some writer's imagination,
Atremble, romantic, disguised. In every thing

A ghostly gesture toward some other. In Yeats's
"The Stare's Nest by My Window" the Catholic soldier
Trundled in his blood, the nestlings fed on grubs,

The heart grown brutal from feeding on fantasies.
The Crusaders killed how many thousands of Jews
Among the thousands of Muslims. I used to know

A high school student who was brilliant at French.
The family she stayed with one summer were very kind
Though their allusions to dirty Jews or Arabs

Did bother her. What curdled her love for their language
Was how unconscious it was, like humming a tune:
"You couldn't wipe them out, they breed like rats."

All the starlings in America are descended
From ones imported because a certain man
Wanted a park with every bird mentioned by Shakespeare.

The birds are a pest, they drive out native species
In the world's rivalrous web of exterminations
And propagating shadows, the net of being.

Eurydice and Stalin

She crossed a bridge, and looking down she saw
The little Georgian boiling in a trench of blood.
He hailed her, and holding up his one good arm

He opened his palm to show her two pulpy seeds
Like droplets—one for each time she lost her life.
Then in a taunting voice he chanted some verses.

Poetry was popular in Hell, the shades
Recited lines they had memorized—forgetful
Even of who they were, but famished for life.

And who was she? The little scoundrel below her
Opened his palm again to show that the seeds
Had multiplied, there was one for every month

He held her child hostage, or each false poem
He extorted from her. He smiled a curse and gestured
As though to offer her a quenching berry.

On certain pages of her printed books
She had glued new handwritten poems to cover
The ones she was ashamed of: now could he want

Credit as her patron, for those thickened pages?
He said she was the canary he had blinded
To make it sing. Her courage, so much birdseed.

Shame, endless revision, inexhaustible art:
The hunchback loves his hump. She crossed the bridge
And wandered across a field of steaming ashes.

Was it a government or an impassioned mob
That tore some poet to pieces? She struggled to recall
The name, and was it herself, a radiant O.

The Forgetting

The forgetting I notice most as I get older is really a form of memory:
The undergrowth of things unknown to you young, that I have forgotten.

Memory of so much crap, jumbled with so much that seems to matter.
Lieutenant Calley. Captain Easy. Mayling Soong. Sibby Sisti.

And all the forgettings that preceded my own: Baghdad, Egypt, Greece,
The Plains, centuries of lootings of antiquities. Obscure atrocities.

Imagine!—a big tent filled with mostly kids, yelling for poetry. In fact
It happened, I was there in New Jersey at the famous poetry show.

I used to wonder, what if the Baseball Hall of Fame overflowed
With too many thousands of greats all in time unremembered?

Hardly anybody can name all eight of their great grandparents.
Can you? Will your children's grandchildren remember your name?

You'll see, you little young jerks: your favorite music and your political
Furors, too, will need to get sorted in dusty electronic corridors.

Robert Pinsky   179

In 1972, Zhou En-Lai was asked the lasting effects of the French
Revolution: "Too soon to tell." Remember?—or was it Mao Tse-Tung?

Poetry made of air strains to reach back to Begats and suspiring
Forward into air, grunting to beget the hungry or overfed Future.

Ezra Pound praises the Emperor who appointed a committee of scholars
To pick the best 450 Noh plays and destroy all the rest, the fascist.

The standup master Stephen Wright says he thinks he suffers from
Both amnesia and déjà vu: "I feel like I have forgotten this before."

Who remembers the arguments when jurors gave Pound the only prize
For poetry awarded by the United States Government? Until then.

I was in the big tent when the guy read his poem about how the Jews
Were warned to get out of the Twin Towers before the planes hit.

The crowd was applauding and screaming, they were happy—it isn't
That they were anti-Semitic, or anything. They just weren't listening. Or

No, they were listening, but that certain way. In it comes, you hear it, and
That selfsame second you swallow it or expel it: an ecstasy of forgetting.

Poem of Disconnected Parts

    At Robben Island the political prisoners studied.
    They coined the motto *Each one Teach one.*

    In Argentina the torturers demanded the prisoners
    Address them always as "*Profesor.*"

    Many of my friends are moved by guilt, but I
    Am a creature of shame, I am ashamed to say.

    Culture the lock, culture the key. Imagination
    That calls boiled sheep heads in the market "Smileys."

The first year at Guantánamo, Abdul Rahim Dost
Incised his Pashto poems into styrofoam cups.

"The Sangomo says in our Zulu culture we do not
Worship our ancestors: we consult them."

Becky is abandoned in 1902 and Rose dies giving
Birth in 1924 and Sylvia falls in 1951.

Still falling still dying still abandoned in 2006
Still nothing finished among the descendants.

I support the War, says the comic, it's just the Troops
I'm against: can't stand those Young People.

Proud of the fallen, proud of her son the bomber.
Ashamed of the government. Skeptical.

After the Klansman was found Not Guilty one juror
Said she just couldn't vote to convict a pastor.

Who do you write for? I write for dead people:
For Emily Dickinson, for my grandfather.

"The Ancestors say the problem with your Knees
Began in your Feet. It could move up your Back."

But later the Americans gave Dost not only paper
And pen but books. Hemingway, Dickens.

Old Aegyptius said, Whoever has called this Assembly,
For whatever reason—that is a good in itself.

O thirsty shades who regard the offering, O stained earth.
There are many fake Sangomos. This one is real.

Coloured prisoners got different meals and could wear
Long pants and underwear, Blacks got only shorts.

No he says he cannot regret the three years in prison:
Otherwise he would not have written those poems.

Robert Pinsky

I have a small-town mind. Like the Greeks and Trojans.
Shame. Pride. Importance of looking bad or good.

Did he see anything like the prisoner on a leash? Yes,
In Afghanistan. In Guantánamo he was isolated.

Our enemies "disassemble" says the President.
Not that anyone at all couldn't mis-speak.

The *profesores* created nicknames for torture devices:
The Airplane. The Frog. Burping the Baby.

Not that those who behead the helpless in the name
Of God or tradition don't also write poetry.

Guilts, metaphors, traditions. Hunger strikes.
Culture the penalty. Culture the escape.

What could your children boast about you? What
Will your father say, down among the shades?

The Sangomo told Marvin, "*You are crushed by some
Weight. Only your own Ancestors can help you.*"

Samurai Song

When I had no roof I made
Audacity my roof. When I had
No supper my eyes dined.

When I had no eyes I listened.
When I had no ears I thought.
When I had no thought I waited.

When I had no father I made
Care my father. When I had
No mother I embraced order.

When I had no friend I made
Quiet my friend. When I had no
Enemy I opposed my body.

When I had no temple I made
My voice my temple. I have
No priest, my tongue is my choir.

When I have no means fortune
Is my means. When I have
Nothing, death will be my fortune.

Need is my tactic, detachment
Is my strategy. When I had
No lover I courted my sleep.

Ode to Meaning

Dire one and desired one,
Savior, sentencer—

In an old allegory you would carry
A chained alphabet of tokens:

Ankh Badge Cross.
Dragon,
Engraved figure guarding a hallowed intaglio,
Jasper kinema of legendary Mind,
Naked omphalos pierced
By quills of rhyme or sense, torah-like: unborn
Vein of will, xenophile
Yearning out of Zero.

Untrusting I court you. Wavering
I seek your face, I read
That Crusoe's knife
Reeked of you, that to defile you
The soldier makes the rabbi spit on the torah.
"I'll drown my book" says Shakespeare.

Drowned walker, revenant.
After my mother fell on her head, she became
More than ever your sworn enemy. She spoke
Sometimes like a poet or critic of forty years later.
Or she spoke of the world as Thersites spoke of the heroes,
"I think they have swallowed one another. I
Would laugh at that miracle."

You also in the laughter, warrior angel:
Your helmet the zodiac, rocket-plumed
Your spear the beggar's finger pointing to the mouth
Your heel planted on the serpent Formulation
Your face a vapor, the wreath of cigarette smoke crowning
Bogart as he winces through it.

You not in the words, not even
Between the words, but a torsion,
A cleavage, a stirring.

You stirring even in the arctic ice,
Even at the dark ocean floor, even
In the cellular flesh of a stone.

Gas. Gossamer. My poker friends
Question your presence
In a poem by me, passing the magazine
One to another.

Not the stone and not the words, you
Like a veil over Arthur's headstone,
The passage from Proverbs he chose
While he was too ill to teach
And still well enough to read, *I was*
Beside the master craftsman
Delighting him day after day, ever
At play in his presence—you

A soothing veil of distraction playing over
Dying Arthur playing in the hospital,
Thumbing the Bible, fuzzy from medication,
Ever courting your presence.
And you the prognosis,
You in the cough.

Gesturer, when is your spur, your cloud?
You in the airport rituals of greeting and parting.
Indicter, who is your claimant?
Bell at the gate. Spiderweb iron bridge.
Cloak, video, aroma, rue, what is your
Elected silence, where was your seed?

What is Imagination
But your lost child born to give birth to you?

Dire one. Desired one.
Savior, sentencer—

Absence,
Or presence ever at play:
Let those scorn you who never
Starved in your dearth. If I
Dare to disparage
Your harp of shadows I taste
Wormwood and motor oil, I pour
Ashes on my head. You are the wound. You
Be the medicine.

To Television

Not a "window on the world"
But as we call you,
A box a tube

Terrarium of dreams and wonders.
Coffer of shades, ordained
Cotillion of phosphors
Or liquid crystal

Homey miracle, tub
Of acquiescence, vein of defiance.
Your patron in the pantheon would be Hermes

Raster dance,
Quick one, little thief, escort
Of the dying and comfort of the sick,

In a blue glow my father and little sister sat
Snuggled in one chair watching you
Their wife and mother was sick in the head
I scorned you and them as I scorned so much

Now I like you best in a hotel room,
Maybe minutes
Before I have to face an audience: behind
The doors of the armoire, box
Within a box—Tom & Jerry, or also brilliant
And reassuring, Oprah Winfrey.

Thank you, for I watched, I watched
Sid Caesar speaking French and Japanese not
Through knowledge but imagination,
His quickness, and Thank you, I watched live
Jackie Robinson stealing

Home, the image—O strung shell—enduring
Fleeter than light like these words we
Remember in: they too are winged
At the helmet and ankles.

The Green Piano

Aeolian. Gratis. Great thunderer, half-ton infant of miracles
Torn free of charge from the universe by my mother's will.
You must have amazed that half-respectable street

Of triple-decker families and rooming-house housepainters
The day that the bole-ankled oversized hams of your legs
Bobbed in procession up the crazy-paved front walk

Embraced by the arms of Mr. Poppik the seltzer man
And Corydon his black-skinned helper, tendering your thighs
Thick as a man up our steps. We are not reptiles:

Even the male body bears nipples, as if to remind us
We are designed for dependence and nutriment, past
Into future. O Europe, they budged your case, its ponderous

Guts of iron and brass, ten kinds of hardwood and felt
Up those heel-pocked risers and treads splintering tinder.
Angelic nurse of clamor, yearner, tinkler, dominator—

O Elephant, you were for me! When the tuner Mr. Otto Van Brunt
Pronounced you excellent despite the cracked sounding board, we
Obeyed him and swabbed your ivories with hydrogen peroxide.

You blocked a doorway and filled most of the living room.
The sofa and chairs dwindled to a ram and ewes, cowering: now,
The colored neighbors could be positive we were crazy and rich,

As we thought the people were who gave you away for the moving
Out of their carriage house—they had painted you the color of pea soup.
The drunk man my mother hired never finished antiquing you

Ivory and umber, so you stood half-done, a throbbing mistreated noble,
Genuine—my mother's swollen livestock of love: lost one, unmastered:
You were the beast she led to the shrine of my genius, mistaken.

Endlessly I bonged according to my own chord system *Humoresque,*
The Talk of the Town, What'd I Say. Then one day they painted you pink.
Pink is how my sister remembers you the Saturday afternoon

When our mother fell on her head, dusty pink as I turn on the bench
In my sister's memory to see them carrying our mother up the last
Steps and into the living room, inaugurating the reign of our confusion.

They sued the builder of the house she fell in, with the settlement
They bought a house at last and one day when I came home from college
You were gone, mahogany breast, who nursed me through those

Years of the Concussion, and there was a crappy little Baldwin Acrosonic
In your place, gleaming, walnut shell. You were gone, despoiled one—
Pink one, forever-green one, white and gold one, comforter, a living soul.

Jersey Rain

Now near the end of the middle stretch of road
What have I learned? Some earthly wiles. An art.
That often I cannot tell good fortune from bad,
That once had seemed so easy to tell apart.

The source of art and woe aslant in wind
Dissolves or nourishes everything it touches.
What roadbank gullies and ruts it doesn't mend
It carves the deeper, boiling tawny in ditches.

It spends itself regardless into the ocean.
It stains and scours and makes things dark or bright:
Sweat of the moon, a shroud of benediction,
The chilly liquefaction of day to night,

The Jersey rain, my rain, soaks all as one:
It smites Metuchen, Rahway, Saddle River,
Fair Haven, Newark, Little Silver, Bayonne.
I feel it churning even in fair weather

Five American Poets

To craze distinction, dry the same as wet.
In ripples of heat the August drought still feeds
Vapors in the sky that swell to drench my state—
The Jersey rain, my rain, in streams and beads

Of indissoluble grudge and aspiration:
Original milk, replenisher of grief,
Descending destroyer, arrowed source of passion,
Silver and black, executioner, font of life.

Ginza Samba

A monosyllabic European called Sax
Invents a horn, walla whirledy wah, a kind of twisted
Brazen clarinet, but with its column of vibrating
Air shaped not in a cylinder but in a cone
Widening ever outward and bawaah spouting
Infinitely upward through an upturned
Swollen golden bell rimmed
Like a gloxinia flowering
In Sax's Belgian imagination

And in the unfathomable matrix
Of mothers and fathers as a genius graven
Humming into the cells of the body
Or cupped in the resonating grail
Of memory changed and exchanged
As in the trading of brasses,
Pearls and ivory, calicos and slaves,
Laborers and girls, two

Cousins in a royal family
Of Niger known as the Birds or Hawks.
In Christendom one cousin's child
Becomes a "favorite negro" ennobled
By decree of the Czar and founds
A great family, a line of generals,
Dandies and courtiers including the poet
Pushkin, killed in a duel concerning
His wife's honor, while the other cousin sails

In the belly of a slaveship to the port
Of Baltimore where she is raped
And dies in childbirth, but the infant
Will marry a Seminole and in the next
Chorus of time their child fathers
A great Hawk or Bird, with many followers
Among them this great-grandchild of the Jewish
Manager of a Pushkin estate, blowing

His American breath out into the wiggly
Tune uncurling its triplets and sixteenths—the Ginza
Samba of breath and brass, the reed
Vibrating as a valve, the aether, the unimaginable
Wires and circuits of an ingenious box
Here in my room in this house built
A hundred years ago while I was elsewhere:

It is like falling in love, the atavistic
Imperative of some one
Voice or face—the skill, the copper filament,
The golden bellful of notes twirling through
Their invisible element from
Rio to Tokyo and back again gathering
Speed in the variations as they tunnel
The twin haunted labyrinths of stirrup
And anvil echoing here in the hearkening
Instrument of my skull.

Poem with Refrains

The opening scene. The yellow, coal-fed fog
Uncurling over the tainted city river,
A young girl rowing and her anxious father
Scavenging for corpses. Funeral meats. The clever
Abandoned orphan. The great athletic killer
Sulking in his tent. As though all stories began
With someone dying.

               When her mother died,
My mother refused to attend the funeral—
In fact, she sulked in her tent all through the year
Of the old lady's dying, I don't know why:
She said, because she loved her mother so much
She couldn't bear to see the way the doctors,
Or her father, or—someone—was letting her mother die.
"Follow your saint, follow with accents sweet;
Haste you, sad notes, fall at her flying feet."

She fogs things up, she scavenges the taint.
Possibly that's the reason I write these poems.

But they did speak: on the phone. Wept and argued,
So fiercely one or the other often cut off
A sentence by hanging up in rage—like lovers,
But all that year she never saw her face.

They lived on the same block, four doors apart.
"Absence my presence is; strangeness my grace;
With them that walk against me is my sun."

"Synagogue" is a word I never heard,
We called it *shul,* the Yiddish word for school.
Elms, terra cotta, the ocean a few blocks east.
"Lay institution": she taught me we didn't think
God lived in it. The rabbi just a teacher.

But what about the hereditary priests,
Descendants of the Cohanes of the Temple,
Like Walter Holtz—I called him Uncle Walter,
When I was small. A big man with a face
Just like a boxer dog or a cartoon sergeant.
She told me whenever he helped a pretty woman
Try on a shoe in his store, he'd touch her calf
And ask her, "How does that feel?" I was too little
To get the point but pretended to understand.
"Desire, be steady; hope is your delight,
An orb wherein no creature can be sorry."

She didn't go to my bar mitzvah, either.
I can't say why: she was there, and then she wasn't.
I looked around before I mounted the steps
To chant that babble and the speech the rabbi wrote
And there she wasn't, and there was Uncle Walter
The Cohane frowning with his doggy face:
"She's missing her own son's *musaf.*" Maybe she just
Doesn't like rituals. Afterwards, she had a reason
I don't remember. I wasn't upset: the truth
Is, I had decided to be the clever orphan
Some time before. By now, it's all a myth.
What is a myth but something that seems to happen
Always for the first time over and over again?
And ten years later, she missed my brother's, too.
I'm sorry: I think it was something about a hat.
"Hot sun, cool fire, tempered with sweet air,
Black shade, fair nurse, shadow my white hair;
Shine, sun; burn, fire; breathe, air, and ease me."

She sees the minister of the Nation of Islam
On television, though she's half-blind in one eye.
His bow tie is lime, his jacket crocodile green.
Vigorously he denounces the Jews who traded in slaves,
The Jews who run the newspapers and the banks.
"I see what this guy is mad about now," she says,
"It must have been some Jew that sold him the suit."
"And the same wind sang and the same wave whitened,
And or ever the garden's last petals were shed,
In the lips that had whispered, the eyes that had lightened."

Five American Poets

But when they unveiled her mother's memorial stone,
Gathered at the graveside one year after the death,
According to custom, while we were standing around
About to begin the prayers, her car appeared.
It was a black car; the ground was deep in snow.
My mother got out and walked toward us, across
The field of gravestones capped with snow, her coat
Black as the car, and they waited to start the prayers
Until she arrived. I think she enjoyed the drama.
I can't remember if she prayed or not,
But that may be the way I'll remember her best:
Dark figure, awaited, attended, aware, apart.
"The present time upon time passëd striketh;
With Phoebus's wandering course the earth is graced.

The air still moves, and by its moving, cleareth;
The fire up ascends, and planets feedeth;
The water passeth on, and all lets weareth;
The earth stands still, yet change of changes breedeth."

House Hour

Now the pale honey of a kitchen light
Burns at an upstairs window, the sash a cross.
Milky daylight moon,
Sky scored by phone lines. Houses in rows
Patient as cows.

Dormers and gables of an immigrant street
In a small city, the wind-worn afternoon
Shading into night.

Robert Pinsky

Hundreds of times before
I have felt it in some district
Of shingle and downspout at just this hour.
The renter walking home from the bus
Carrying a crisp bag. Maybe a store
Visible at the corner, neon at dusk.
Macaroni mist fogging the glass.

Unwilled, seductive as music, brief
As dusk itself, the forgotten mirror
Brushed for dozens of years
By the same gray light, the same shadows
Of soffit and beam end, a reef
Of old snow glowing along the walk.

If I am hollow, or if I am heavy with longing, the same:
The ponderous houses of siding,
Fir framing, horsehair plaster, fired bricks
In a certain light, changing nothing, but touching
Those separate hours of the past
And now at this one time
Of day touching this one, last spokes
Of light silvering the attic dust.

From the Childhood of Jesus

One Saturday morning he went to the river to play.
He modelled twelve sparrows out of the river clay

And scooped a clear pond, with a dam of twigs and mud.
Around the pond he set the birds he had made,

Evenly as the hours. Jesus was five. He smiled,
As a child would who had made a little world

Of clear still water and clay beside a river.
But a certain Jew came by, a friend of his father,

And he scolded the child and ran at once to Joseph,
Saying, "Come see how your child has profaned the Sabbath,

Making images at the river on the Day of Rest."
So Joseph came to the place and took his wrist

And told him, "Child, you have offended the Word."
Then Jesus freed the hand that Joseph held

And clapped his hands and shouted to the birds
To go away. They raised their beaks at his words

And breathed and stirred their feathers and flew away.
The people were frightened. Meanwhile, another boy,

The son of Annas the scribe, had idly taken
A branch of driftwood and leaning against it had broken

The dam and muddied the little pond and scattered
The twigs and stones. Then Jesus was angry and shouted,

"Unrighteous, impious, ignorant, what did the water
Do to harm you? Now you are going to wither

The way a tree does, you shall bear no fruit
And no leaves, you shall wither down to the root."

At once, the boy was all withered. His parents moaned,
The Jews gasped, Jesus began to leave, then turned

And prophesied, his child's face wet with tears:
"Twelve times twelve times twelve thousands of years

Before these heavens and this earth were made,
The Creator set a jewel in the throne of God

With Hell on the left and Heaven to the right,
The Sanctuary in front, and behind, an endless night

Endlessly fleeing a Torah written in flame.
And on that jewel in the throne, God wrote my name."

Then Jesus left and went into Joseph's house.
The family of the withered one also left the place,

Carrying him home. The Sabbath was nearly over.
By dusk, the Jews were all gone from the river.

Small creatures came from the undergrowth to drink
And foraged in the shadows along the bank.

Alone in his cot in Joseph's house, the Son
Of Man was crying himself to sleep. The moon

Rose higher, the Jews put out their lights and slept,
And all was calm and as it had been, except

In the agitated household of the scribe Annas,
And high in the dark, where unknown even to Jesus

The twelve new sparrows flew aimlessly through the night,
Not blinking or resting, as if never to alight.

The Hearts

The legendary muscle that wants and grieves,
The organ of attachment, the pump of thrills
And troubles, clinging in stubborn colonies

Like pulpy shore-life battened on a jetty.
Slashed by the little deaths of sleep and pleasure,
They swell in the nurturing spasms of the waves,

Sucking to cling; and even in death itself—
Baked, frozen—they shrink to grip the granite harder.
"Rid yourself of attachments and aversions"—

But in her father's orchard, already, he says
He'd like to be her bird, and she says: Sweet, yes,
Yet I should kill thee with much cherishing,

Showing that she knows already—as Art Pepper,
That first time he takes heroin, already knows
That he will go to prison, and knows he'll suffer

And knows he needs to have it, or die; and the one
Who makes the General lose the world for love
Lets him say, *Would I had never seen her*, but Oh!

Says Enobarbus, Then you would have missed
A wonderful piece of work, which left unseen
Would bring less glory to your travels. Among

The creatures in the rock-torn surf, a wave
Of agitation, a gasp. A scholar quips,
Shakespeare was almost certainly homosexual,

Bisexual, or heterosexual, the sonnets
Provide no evidence on the matter. He writes
Romeo an extravagant speech on tears,

In the Italian manner, his teardrops cover
His chamber window, says the boy, he calls them crystals,
Inanely, and sings them to Juliet with his heart:

The almost certainly invented heart
Which Buddha denounces, in its endless changes
Forever jumping and moving, like an ape.

Over the poor beast's head the crystal fountain
Crashes illusions, the cold salt spume of pain
And meaningless distinction, as Buddha says,

But here in the crystal shower mouths are open
To sing, it is Lee Andrews and The Hearts
In 1957, singing *I sit in my room*

Looking out at the rain, My teardrops are
Like crystals, they cover my windowpane, the turns
Of these illusions we make become their glory:

To Buddha every distinct thing is illusion
And becoming is destruction, but still we sing
In the shower. I do. In the beginning God drenched

The Emptiness with images: the potter
Crosslegged at his wheel in Benares market
Making mud cups, another cup each second

Tapering up between his fingers, one more
To sell the tea-seller at a penny a dozen,
And tea a penny a cup. The customers smash

The empties, and waves of traffic grind the shards
To mud for new cups, in turn; and I keep one here
Next to me: holding it a while from out of the cloud

Of dust that rises from the shattered pieces,
The risen dust alive with fire, then settled
And soaked and whirling again on the wheel that turns

And looks on the world as on another cloud,
On everything the heart can grasp and throw away
As a passing cloud, with even Enlightenment

Itself another image, another cloud
To break and churn a salt foam over the heart
Like an anemone that sucks at clouds and makes

Itself with clouds and sings in clouds and covers
Its windowpane with clouds that blur and melt,
Until one clings and holds—as once in the Temple

In the time before the Temple was destroyed
A young priest saw the seraphim of the Lord:
Each had six wings, with two they covered their faces,

With two they covered their legs and feet, with two
They darted and hovered like dragonflies or perched
Like griffins in the shadows near the ceiling—

These are the visions, too barbarous for heaven
And too preposterous for belief on earth,
God sends to taunt his prophet with the truth

No one can see, that leads to who knows where.
A seraph took a live coal from the altar
And seared the prophet's lips, and so he spoke.

As the record ends, a coda in retard:
The Hearts in a shifting velvety *ah*, and *ah*
Prolonged again, and again as Lee Andrews

Reaches *ah* high for *I have to gain Faith, Hope*
And Charity, God only knows the girl
Who will love me—Oh! if we only could

Start over again! Then The Hearts chant the chords
Again a final time, *ah* and the record turns
Through all the music, and on into silence again.

The Want Bone

The tongue of the waves tolled in the earth's bell.
Blue rippled and soaked in the fire of blue.
The dried mouthbones of a shark in the hot swale
Gaped on nothing but sand on either side.

The bone tasted of nothing and smelled of nothing,
A scalded toothless harp, uncrushed, unstrung.
The joined arcs made the shape of birth and craving
And the welded-open shape kept mouthing O.

Ossified cords held the corners together
In groined spirals pleated like a summer dress.
But where was the limber grin, the gash of pleasure?
Infinitesimal mouths bore it away,

The beach scrubbed and etched and pickled it clean.
But O I love you it sings, my little my country
My food my parent my child I want you my own
My flower my fin my life my lightness my O.

An Old Man

after Cavafy

Back in a corner, alone in the clatter and babble
An old man sits with his head bent over a table
And his newspaper in front of him, in the café.

Sour with old age, he ponders a dreary truth—
How little he enjoyed the years when he had youth,
Good looks and strength and clever things to say.

He knows he's quite old now: he feels it, he sees it,
And yet the time when he was young seems—was it?
Yesterday. How quickly, how quickly it slipped away.

Now he sees how Discretion has betrayed him,
And how stupidly he let the liar persuade him
With phrases: *Tomorrow. There's plenty of time. Some day.*

He recalls the pull of impulses he suppressed,
The joy he sacrificed. Every chance he lost
Ridicules his brainless prudence a different way.

But all these thoughts and memories have made
The old man dizzy. He falls asleep, his head
Resting on the table in the noisy café.

Shirt

The back, the yoke, the yardage. Lapped seams,
The nearly invisible stitches along the collar
Turned in a sweatshop by Koreans or Malaysians

Gossiping over tea and noodles on their break
Or talking money or politics while one fitted
This armpiece with its overseam to the band

Of cuff I button at my wrist. The presser, the cutter,
The wringer, the mangle. The needle, the union,
The treadle, the bobbin. The code. The infamous blaze

At the Triangle Factory in nineteen-eleven.
One hundred and forty six died in the flames
On the ninth floor, no hydrants, no fire escapes—

The witness in a building across the street
Who watched how a young man helped a girl to step
Up to the window sill, then held her out

Away from the masonry wall and let her drop.
And then another. As if he were helping them up
To enter a streetcar, and not eternity.

A third before he dropped her put her arms
Around his neck and kissed him. Then he held
Her into space, and dropped her. Almost at once

He stepped to the sill himself, his jacket flared
And fluttered up from his shirt as he came down,
Air filling up the legs of his gray trousers—

Like Hart Crane's Bedlamite, "shrill shirt ballooning."
Wonderful how the pattern matches perfectly
Across the placket and over the twin bar-tacked

Corners of both pockets, like a strict rhyme
Or a major chord. Prints, plaids, checks,
Houndstooth, Tattersall, Madras. The clan tartans

Invented by mill-owners inspired by the hoax of Ossian,
To control their savage Scottish workers, tamed
By a fabricated heraldry: MacGregor,

Bailey, MacMartin. The kilt, devised for workers
To wear among the dusty clattering looms.
Weavers, carders, spinners. The loader,

The docker, the navvy. The planter, the picker, the sorter
Sweating at her machine in a litter of cotton
As slaves in calico headrags sweated in fields:

George Herbert, your descendant is a Black
Lady in South Carolina, her name is Irma
And she inspected my shirt. Its color and fit

And feel and its clean smell have satisfied
Both her and me. We have culled its cost and quality
Down to the buttons of simulated bone,

The buttonholes, the sizing, the facing, the characters
Printed in black on neckband and tail. The shape,
The label, the labor, the color, the shade. The shirt.

At Pleasure Bay

In the willows along the river at Pleasure Bay
A catbird singing, never the same phrase twice.
Here under the pines a little off the road
In 1927 the Chief of Police
And Mrs. W. killed themselves together,
Sitting in a roadster. Ancient unshaken pilings
And underwater chunks of still-mortared brick

In shapes like bits of puzzle strew the bottom
Where the landing was for Price's Hotel and Theater.
And here's where boats blew two blasts for the keeper
To shunt the iron swing-bridge. He leaned on the gears
Like a skipper in the hut that housed the works
And the bridge moaned and turned on its middle pier
To let them through. In the middle of the summer
Two or three cars might wait for the iron trusswork
Winching aside, with maybe a child to notice
A name on the stern in black-and-gold on white,
Sandpiper, Patsy Ann, Do Not Disturb,
The Idler. If a boat was running whiskey,
The bridge clanged shut behind it as it passed
And opened up again for the Coast Guard cutter
Slowly as a sundial, and always jammed halfway.
The roadbed whole, but opened like a switch,
The river pulling and coursing between the piers.
Never the same phrase twice, the catbird filling
The humid August evening near the inlet
With borrowed music that he melds and changes.
Dragonflies and sandflies, frogs in the rushes, two bodies
Not moving in the open car among the pines,
A sliver of story. The tenor at Price's Hotel,
In clown costume, unfurls the sorrow gathered
In ruffles at his throat and cuffs, high quavers
That hold like splashes of light on the dark water,
The aria's closing phrases, changed and fading.
And after a gap of quiet, cheers and applause
Audible in the houses across the river,
Some in the audience weeping as if they had melted
Inside the music. Never the same. In Berlin
The daughter of an English lord, in love
With Adolf Hitler, whom she has met. She is taking
Possession of the apartment of a couple,
Elderly well-off Jews. They survive the war
To settle here in the Bay, the old lady
Teaches piano, but the whole world swivels
And gapes at their feet as the girl and a high-up Nazi
Examine the furniture, the glass, the pictures,
The elegant story that was theirs and now

Is a part of hers. A few months later the English
Enter the war and she shoots herself in a park,
An addled, upper-class girl, her life that passes
Into the lives of others or into a place.
The taking of lives—the Chief and Mrs. W.
Took theirs to stay together, as local ghosts.
Last flurries of kisses, the revolver's barrel,
Shivers of a story that a child might hear
And half remember, voices in the rushes,
A singing in the willows. From across the river,
Faint quavers of music, the same phrase twice and again,
Ranging and building. Over the high new bridge
The flashing of traffic homeward from the racetrack,
With one boat chugging under the arches, outward
Unnoticed through Pleasure Bay to the open sea.
Here's where the people stood to watch the theater
Burn on the water. All that night the fireboats
Kept playing their spouts of water into the blaze.
In the morning, smoking pilasters and beams.
Black smell of char for weeks, the ruin already
Soaking back into the river. After you die
You hover near the ceiling above your body
And watch the mourners awhile. A few days more
You float above the heads of the ones you knew
And watch them through a twilight. As it grows darker
You wander off and find your way to the river
And wade across. On the other side, night air,
Willows, the smell of the river, and a mass
Of sleeping bodies all along the bank,
A kind of singing from among the rushes
Calling you further forward in the dark.
You lie down and embrace one body, the limbs
Heavy with sleep reach eagerly up around you
And you make love until your soul brims up
And burns free out of you and shifts and spills
Down over into that other body, and you
Forget the life you had and begin again
On the same crossing—maybe as a child who passes
Through the same place. But never the same way twice.
Here in the daylight, the catbird in the willows,

The new café, with a terrace and a landing,
Frogs in the cattails where the swing-bridge was—
Here's where you might have slipped across the water
When you were only a presence, at Pleasure Bay.

ABC

Any body can die, evidently. Few
Go happily, irradiating joy,

Knowledge, love. Many
Need oblivion, painkillers,
Quickest respite.

Sweet time unafflicted,
Various world:

X=your zenith.

XYZ

The cross the fork the zigzag—a few straight lines
For pain, quandary and evasion, the last of signs.

Memorial

J.E. and N.M.S.

Here lies a man. And here, a girl. They live
In the kind of artificial life we give

To birds or statues: imagining what they feel,
Or that like birds the dead each had one call,

Repeated, or a gesture that suspends
Their being in a forehead or the hands.

A man comes whistling from a house. The screen
Snaps shut behind him. Though there is no man

And no house, memory sends him to get tools
From a familiar shed, and so he strolls

Through summer shade to work on the family car.
He is my uncle, and fresh home from the war

With nothing for me to remember him doing yet.
The clock of the cancer ticks in his body, or not,

Depending if it is there, or waits. The search
Of memory gains and fails like surf: the porch

And trim are painted cream, the shakes are stained.
The shadows could be painted (so little wind

Is blowing there) or stains on the crazy-paving
Of the front walk... Or now, the shadows are moving:

Another house, unrelated; a woman says,
Is this your special boy, and the girl says yes,

Moving her hand in mine. The clock in her, too—
As someone told me a month or two ago,

Months after it finally took her. A public building
Is where the house was: though a surf, unyielding

And sickly, seethes and eddies at the stones
Of the foundation. The dead are made of bronze,

But living they were like birds with clocklike hearts—
Unthinkable how much pain the tiny parts

Of even the smallest bird might yet contain.
We become larger than life in how much pain

Our bodies may encompass ... all Titans in that,
Or heroic statues. Although there is no heat

Brimming in the fixed, memorial summer, the brows
Of lucid metals sweat a faint warm haze

As I try to think the pain I never saw.
Though there is no pain there, the small birds draw

Together in crowds above the houses—and cry
Over the surf: as if there were a day,

Memorial, marked on the calendar for dread
And pain and loss—although among the dead

Are no hurts, but only emblematic things;
No hospital beds, but a lifting of metal wings.

Robert Pinsky

The Figured Wheel

The figured wheel rolls through shopping malls and prisons,
Over farms, small and immense, and the rotten little downtowns.
Covered with symbols, it mills everything alive and grinds
The remains of the dead in the cemeteries, in unmarked graves and oceans.

Sluiced by salt water and fresh, by pure and contaminated rivers,
By snow and sand, it separates and recombines all droplets and grains,
Even the infinite sub-atomic particles crushed under the illustrated,
Varying treads of its wide circumferential track.

Spraying flecks of tar and molten rock it rumbles
Through the Antarctic station of American sailors and technicians,
And shakes the floors and windows of whorehouses for diggers and smelters
From Bethany, Pennsylvania to a practically nameless, semi-penal New Town

In the mineral-rich tundra of the Soviet northernmost settlements.
Artists illuminate it with pictures and incised mottoes
Taken from the Ten-Thousand Stories and the Register of True Dramas.
They hang it with colored ribbons and with bells of many pitches.

With paints and chisels and moving lights they record
On its rotating surface the elegant and terrifying doings
Of the inhabitants of the Hundred Pantheons of major Gods
Disposed in iconographic stations at hub, spoke and concentric bands,

And also the grotesque demi-Gods, Hopi gargoyles and Ibo dryads.
They cover it with wind-chimes and electronic instruments
That vibrate as it rolls to make an all-but-unthinkable music,
So that the wheel hums and rings as it turns through the births of stars

And through the dead-world of bomb, fireblast and fallout
Where only a few doomed races of insects fumble in the smoking grasses.
It is Jesus oblivious to hurt turning to give words to the unrighteous,
And is also Gogol's feeding pig that without knowing it eats a baby chick

And goes on feeding. It is the empty armor of My Cid, clattering
Into the arrows of the credulous unbelievers, a metal suit
Like the lost astronaut revolving with his useless umbilicus
Through the cold streams, neither energy nor matter, that agitate

The cold, cyclical dark, turning and returning.
Even in the scorched and frozen world of the dead after the holocaust
The wheel as it turns goes on accreting ornaments.
Scientists and artists festoon it from the grave with brilliant

Toys and messages, jokes and zodiacs, tragedies conceived
From among the dreams of the unemployed and the pampered,
The listless and the tortured. It is hung with devices
By dead masters who have survived by reducing themselves magically

To tiny organisms, to wisps of matter, crumbs of soil,
Bits of dry skin, microscopic flakes, which is why they are called "great,"
In their humility that goes on celebrating the turning
Of the wheel as it rolls unrelentingly over

A cow plodding through car-traffic on a street in Iasi,
And over the haunts of Robert Pinsky's mother and father
And wife and children and his sweet self
Which he hereby unwillingly and inexpertly gives up, because it is

There, figured and pre-figured in the nothing-transfiguring wheel.

From the Last Canto of Paradise

Paradiso XXXIII, 46–48, 52–66

As I drew nearer to the end of all desire,
I brought my longing's ardor to a final height,
Just as I ought. My vision, becoming pure,

Entered more and more the beam of that high light
That shines on its own truth. From then, my seeing
Became too large for speech, which fails at a sight

Beyond all boundaries, at memory's undoing—
As when the dreamer sees and after the dream
The passion endures, imprinted on his being

Though he can't recall the rest. I am the same:
Inside my heart, although my vision is almost
Entirely faded, droplets of its sweetness come

The way the sun dissolves the snow's crust—
The way, in the wind that stirrred the light leaves,
The oracle that the Sibyl wrote was lost.

from *The Paris Review* interview, "The Art of Poetry, no. 76: Robert Pinsky" (Issue 144, Fall 1997). Conducted by Ben Downing and Dan Kunitz

INTERVIEWER   From your essay "Some Passages of Isaiah": "Grandpa Dave stood for the immense beauty and power of idolatry, the adoration of all that can be made and enjoyed by the human body." Does your focus on *making* in poetry continue a family line of utility, to shape something actual?

PINSKY   When I was quite young, we were more or less poor, so pragmatism had considerable urgency.

Dave, my father's father, had a certain swagger, glamour and capacity for violence. A bartender, said to be good at keeping the peace. I guess violence sometimes has utility. My other grandfather, Morris, was a window-washer, tailor, putterer. He could fix clocks and motors; he courted his wife by dazzling her with a motorcycle. (She was married to someone else at the time.) He tuned up his own car, replaced the brake linings and so forth.

INTERVIEWER   Do you consider that background an advantage to you as a writer?

PINSKY   Both grandfathers partook of the pleasures of the marketplace, a term that maybe connotes capitalism. But there's a more ancient sense of the marketplace or agora: the public space, where people see each other when they venture out—the shared home away from the family hearth. The *Odyssey* celebrates not only coming home but also going out: risking the sea, challenging Poseidon to see what deals you can make, what you can get, achieve or learn. Laboring, mercantile, small-town, lower-middle-class life respects not only gain, but also exchange. I suppose something in my work as a writer may extend that ethic—or react against it.

INTERVIEWER   You've also shown affection for the language of trade, notably in your poem "Shirt."

PINSKY   The tenants in our building and the rooming houses on either side were housepainters, railroad workers, masons, pizza cooks: each craft with its specialized vocabulary. In Summer, horse trainers, grooms, maybe one or two jockeys. My father was an optician; a technical jargon went with that job, too.

But it's important to recognize that there's a boring, sometimes oppressive cult of competence in American life and literature—especially competence in basic, even primitive skills. There's a certain amount of baloney, for instance, about fishing and hunting—which is not to say that those cannot be written about well, also.

INTERVIEWER   In your essay "American Poetry and American Life," you salute what you term our poetry's "heteroglossia," its force of contrast between high and low diction. Do you try in your own work to include as many levels of speech as possible?

PINSKY   I would like to keep and somehow unify all the different kinds of experience, and therefore all the different kinds of language, I've ever known. I grew up in a neighborhood that you might call—as my mother did, complaining endlessly about having to live there—a slum. It was not monochromatic. There was a lot of variety culturally, ethnically, in class and in kind of education. People spoke with various accents. I'd like to write a poetry that pretends neither that I've been a professor all my life, nor that I'm really a streetboy. A poetry that doesn't pretend I've never watched television, nor that I've never been to graduate school.

I love how some poems—not only by Williams, but by Dickinson or Ben Jonson, too—constantly modulate precise answers to the questions, "Who says this?" or "Who's talking?" The answer varies constantly: the voice proclaiming "That is no country for old men" is subtly different from the one that lists "What is past, or passing, or to come." The idiom flexes and responds like an oscilloscope: not just the plain style, or the grand style or the Eurekan style, but like a human face in conversation: always changing and always itself.

At optimal heat and pressure, the distinction between "high" and "low" language breaks down: those are unsatisfactory approximations for describing the flow of idiom. Is *strewn* high or low? It's a word roofers use, and Milton. A hardware clerk says, "You could buy one of these devices to spread the fertilizer, or you can just strew it broadcast"—demonstrating that *broadcast* wasn't coined during the Industrial Revolution, or for Marconi. Farmers walk through the fields with a sack slung over one shoulder, to broadcast seed by hand. Obscenities are low, but *fuck*, that very old word, perhaps contains a tinge of loftiness by virtue of being archaic. Is *mullion* the mullion of Sir Kenneth Clark describing a church, or is it the mullion of a carpenter saying, "Shit, the goddam mullions are too fucking short. We need to cut some more"?

INTERVIEWER   Two quotes: you say in the first line of "Long Branch, New Jersey" that "Everything is regional"; and in *Poetry and the World*, "to make one's native place illustrious is an acceptable ancient form of claiming personal significance." Do you feel lucky to come from a place that can be described—as you yourself do—as a microcosm?

PINSKY   In principle, I don't believe anyone's experience is rich or poor in itself: we are all in history. We are in it at the shopping mall exactly as much as or as little as when we are in Tuscany. The mall and Florence, equally, are outcomes of history. The challenge to our historical perception is merely more egregious in some locales than others.

Long Branch does have considerable historical interest—right on its surface. You could argue that in Long Branch the modern idea of celebrity was born, in the late nineteenth century. The town, fairly close to New York by boat or road, was a more raffish resort than Newport and Saratoga Springs, where the social elite summered. Long Branch was for patent-medicine tycoons and theater people: lower class, in those days before money and entertainment conferred the status they do today. President Grant loved Long Branch, which suited his rough style. Diamond Jim Brady vacationed there with Lillian Russell: a raw, less European-style elite than Newport's. The Long Branch social level evolved a hundred years later—with "high society" dead and gone—into its successor in *People* magazine. At the Museum of Fine Arts in Boston, there's a splendid Winslow Homer painting of women with parasols on the bluffs above the beach, entitled "Long Branch, New Jersey."

INTERVIEWER   How conscious were you of all that when you lived there?

PINSKY Hardly at all! Or not until seventh or eighth grade, when we studied Long Branch history, reading Judge Alton Evans's WPA book *Entertaining a Nation*. And I suppose people did talk about history, some. The downtown hotel was named the Garfield–Grant.

Other kinds of history, too, odd survivals. I grew up in an old part of Long Branch, near Flanagan's Field, where a circus visited annually. Every summer, elephants, clowns, girls in tights standing on horses, all paraded right by my house. Lions in wheeled cages. We kids would work for tickets, doing tasks like setting up chairs: tantalizingly close to the mythology of running away with the circus. Once, snooping in an alley between tents, I encountered a family of midgets. The father, with slicked-down yellow hair, in an immaculate white suit, resembled a little boy going to his first communion. Seeing me gawking, he said (approximately): "Who let these fucking son of a bitch, goddamn cocksucking kids in here. Get your god damn fucking asses the Hell out of here!"—really virtuoso profanity in a high-pitched voice, terrifying.

The midget, the vanished tradition of carny and circus jargon, the European roots and gypsy slang—that man cussing me out was the fading voice of all that history. A few years later, everyone was watching television.

INTERVIEWER Did you have a religious upbringing?

PINSKY In a way. My parents were nominally Orthodox Jews, but they were of an assimilated, secular generation, definitely not the black suit and sidelocks idea. My father was a locally famous athlete, voted Best Looking Boy in his high-school yearbook. They didn't go to synagogue except on High Holidays. Sometimes not even then.

But we kept kosher; I didn't taste ham until I was in college. A hamburger and a milkshake together: nearly equivalent to some bizarre sexual practice! They sent me to Hebrew school, but all kinds of falling-off, ambiguity and compromise went back before their generation—went back forever, you might say.

INTERVIEWER And what was your reaction to that kind of conflict and ambiguity?

PINSKY Restless, I suppose.

Five American Poets

SELECT BIBLIOGRAPHY

Robert Hass

Poetry

Field Guide (Yale: Yale University Press, 1973)
Praise (New York: Ecco Press, 1979; Manchester: Carcanet Press, 1981)
Human Wishes (New York: Ecco Press, 1989)
Sun Under Wood (New York: Ecco Press, 1997)
Time and Materials (New York: Ecco/HarperCollins, 2007)
The Apple Trees at Olema: New and Selected Poems (New York: Ecco/Harper Collins, 2010)

Prose

Twentieth Century Pleasures: Prose on Poetry (New York: Ecco Press, 1984)
Now and Then: The Poet's Choice Columns, 1997–99 (Berkeley: Counterpoint, 2006)

Translations

Czesław Miłosz, *The Separate Notebooks* (New York: Ecco Press, 1984), with Robert Pinsky and Renata Gorczynski
Czesław Miłosz, *Unattainable Earth* (New York: Ecco Press, 1986), with the author
Czesław Miłosz, *Collected Poems* (New York: Ecco Press, 1989), with the author and various hands
Czesław Miłosz, *Provinces* (New York: Ecco Press, 1991; Manchester: Carcanet Press, 1993), with the author
The Essential Haiku: Versions of Bashō, Buson, and Issa (New York: Ecco Press, 1994)
Czesław Miłosz, *Facing the River* (New York: Ecco Press, 1995), with the author
Czesław Miłosz, *A Roadside Dog* (New York: Ecco Press, 1998), with the author
Czesław Miłosz, *A Treatise on Poetry* (New York: Ecco Press, 2001), with the author

Czesław Miłosz, *New and Collected Poems* (New York: Ecco Press, 2002), with the author and various hands

Czesław Miłosz, *Second Space* (New York: Ecco Press, 2004), with the author

Anthologies

Robinson Jeffers, *Rock and Hawk: Selected Shorter Poems* (New York: Random House, 1988), edited with an introduction by Robert Hass

Tomas Tranströmer, *Selected Poems, 1954–84* (New York: Ecco Press, 1988), translated by various hands and edited by Robert Hass

Into the Garden: A Wedding Anthology (New York: HarperCollins, 1993), ed. Robert Hass and Stephen Mitchell

Poet's Choice: Poems for Everyday Life (New York: Ecco Press, 1998), ed. Robert Hass

American Poetry: The Twentieth Century, vols 1 and 2 (New York: Library of America, 2001), with John Hollander, Carolyn Kizer, Nathaniel Mackey and Marjorie Perloff

The Best American Poetry 2001 (New York: Scribner, 2002), ed. Robert Hass

The Addison Street Anthology: Berkeley's Poetry Walk (Berkeley: Heyday Books, 2004), ed. Jessica Fisher and Robert Hass

Czesław Miłosz, *Selected Poems* (New York: Ecco Press, 2006), ed. Robert Hass

John Matthias

Poetry

Bucyrus (Chicago: Swallow Press, 1970)

Turns (Chicago: Swallow Press, 1975)

Crossing (Chicago: Swallow Press, 1979)

Bathory & Lermontov (Ahus, Sweden: Kalejdoskop, 1980)

Northern Summer (Chicago: Swallow Press, 1984)

A Gathering of Ways (Athens, OH: Swallow Press, 1991)

Beltane at Aphelion: Longer Poems (Athens, OH: Swallow Press, 1995)

Swimming at Midnight: Selected Shorter Poems (Athens, OH: Swallow Press, 1995)

Pages: New Poems & Cuttings (Athens, OH: Swallow Press, 2000)

Working Progress, Working Title (Cambridge, UK: Salt Publishing, 2002)

Swell & Variations on The Song of Songs (Chicago: Momotombito, 2003)

New Selected Poems (Cambridge, UK: Salt Publishing, 2004)

Kedging (Cambridge, UK: Salt Publishing, 2007)

Translations
Contemporary Swedish Poetry (Athens, OH: Swallow Press, 1980), with Göran Printz-Påhlson
Jan Östergren, *Rainmaker* (Athens, OH: Swallow Press, 1983), with Göran Printz-Påhlson
The Battle of Kosovo (Athens, OH: Swallow Press, 1987), with Vladeta Vučković
Jesper Svenbro, *Three-toed Gull: Selected Poems* (Evanston: Northwestern, 2003), with Lars-Håkan Svensson

Editions
23 Modern British Poets (Chicago: Swallow Press, 1971)
Introducing David Jones (London: Faber and Faber, 1980)
David Jones: Man and Poet (Orono: National Poetry Foundation, 1990)
Selected Works of David Jones (Orono: National Poetry Foundation, 1992)
Notre Dame Review: The First Ten Years (South Bend: Notre Dame University Press, 2009), with William O'Rourke

Criticism
Reading Old Friends (Albany: SUNY Press, 1992)

James McMichael

Poetry
Against the Falling Evil (Chicago: Swallow Press, 1971)
The Lover's Familiar (Boston: David R. Godine, 1978)
Four Good Things (Boston: Houghton Mifflin, 1980)
Each in a Place Apart (Chicago: Chicago University Press, 1994)
The World at Large: New and Selected Poems, 1971–1996 (Chicago: Chicago University Press, 1996)
Capacity (New York: Farrar, Straus and Giroux, 2006)

Prose
The Style of the Short Poem (Belmont: Wadsworth, 1967)
"Ulysses" and Justice (Princeton: Princeton University Press, 1991)

John Peck

Poetry

Shagbark (Indianapolis: Bobbs-Merrill, 1972)

The Broken Blockhouse Wall (Boston: David R. Godine, 1979; Manchester: Carcanet Press, 1979)

Poems and Translations of Hī-Lö (Manchester: Carcanet Press, 1991; New York: Sheep Meadow, 1993)

Argura (Manchester: Carcanet Press, 1993)

Selva Morale (Manchester: Carcanet Press, 1995)

M and Other Poems (Evanston: Northwestern University Press, 1996)

Inizia: Poems Yoked at Yuletide (Magnolia MA: Rhino Editions, 2001) [*hors de commerce*]

Collected Shorter Poems 1966–1996 (Manchester: Carcanet Press, 1999; Evanston: Northwestern University Press, 2003)

Red Strawberry Leaf, Selected Poems 1994–2001 (Chicago: University of Chicago Press, 2005)

Prose

Essays on Guy Davenport, Donald Davie, Hilda Doolittle, Homer and Vietnam War poetry, David Jones, C.G. Jung, Robert Lowell, John Matthias, Christopher Merrill, George Oppen, and Ezra Pound.

Translations

Oscar Milosz, poems and prose, in *The Noble Traveler: The Life and Writings of O. V. de L. Milosz* (West Stockbridge, MA: Lindisfarne Press, 1985), ed. Christopher Bamford

Euripides, *Orestes* (New York: Oxford University Press, 1995), co-translated with Frank Nisetich

C.G. Jung, *Liber Novus, or Jung's Red Book* (New York: Norton, 2009), co-translated with Mark Kyburz and Sonu Shamdasani

Other

Poets Talking: The 'Poet of the Month' Interviews from BBC Radio 3 (Manchester: Carcanet Press, 1994), ed. Clive Wilmer. Interview

Robert Pinsky

Poetry
Sadness and Happiness (Princeton: Princeton University Press, 1975)

An Explanation of America (Princeton: Princeton University Press, 1979; Manchester: Carcanet Press, 1979)

History of My Heart (New York: Ecco Press, 1984)

The Want Bone (New York: Ecco Press, 1990)

The Figured Wheel: New and Collected Poems, 1966–1996 (New York: Farrar, Straus and Giroux, 1996; Manchester: Carcanet Press, 1996)

Jersey Rain (New York: Farrar, Straus and Giroux, 2000)

First Things to Hand (Louisville: Sarabande Books, 2006)

Gulf Music (New York: Farrar, Straus and Giroux, 2007)

Prose
Landor's Poetry (Chicago: Chicago University Press, 1968)

The Situation of Poetry: Contemporary Poetry and Its Traditions (Princeton: Princeton University Press, 1976)

Poetry and the World (New York: Ecco Press, 1988)

The Sounds of Poetry (New York: Farrar, Straus and Giroux, 1998)

Democracy, Culture, and the Voice of Poetry (Princeton: Princeton University Press, 2002)

The Life of David (New York: Schocken, 2005)

Thousands of Broadways (Chicago: Chicago University Press, 2009)

Translations
Czesław Miłosz, *The Separate Notebooks* (New York: Ecco Press, 1984), co-translated with Robert Hass and the author

The Inferno of Dante: A New Verse Translation (New York: Farrar, Straus and Giroux, 1994)

Anthologies
The Handbook of Heartbreak (New York: Rob Weisbach Books, 1998)

Americans' Favorite Poems (New York: Norton, 2000), with Maggie Dietz

Poems to Read (New York: Norton, 2002), with Maggie Dietz

An Invitation to Poetry (New York: Norton, 2004), with Maggie Dietz

Essential Pleasures: Poems to Read Aloud (New York: Norton, 2009)

Other

Mindwheel: An Electronic Novel (California: Synapse and Broderbund, 1984)

Henry David Thoreau, *Cape Cod* (Princeton: Princeton University Press, 1988), introduction by Robert Pinsky

The Paris Review, "The Art of Poetry, no. 76: Robert Pinsky" (Issue 144, Fall 1997), interview

Talking With Poets (New York: Handsel Books, 2002), interview

William Carlos Williams: *Selected Poems* (New York: Library of America, 2004), ed. Robert Pinsky

INDEX OF TITLES

INDEX OF FIRST LINES

ACKNOWLEDGEMENTS

ROBERT HASS

'Heroic Simile', 'Meditation at Lagunitas', 'The Yellow Bicycle', 'The Origin of Cities', 'The Beginning of September', 'Like Three Fair Branches from One Root Deriv'd' and 'Transparent Garments' from *Praise* (Manchester: Carcanet Press, 1981). Copyright © 1981 by Robert Hass. 'Privilege of Being', 'Churchyard', 'Conversion', 'Human Wishes', 'The Apple Trees at Olema', 'Misery and Splendor', 'Cuttings', 'Santa Barbara Road', 'A Story about the Body', 'Spring Drawing', 'Late Spring', '*Rusia en 1931*' and 'Spring Drawing 2' from *Human Wishes* by Robert Hass. Copyright © 1989 by Robert Hass. Reprinted by permission of HarperCollins Publishers. 'Faint Music' and 'The Seventh Night' from *Sun under Wood: New Poems* by Robert Hass. Copyright © 1996 by Robert Hass. Reprinted by permission of HarperCollins Publishers (Ecco Press). 'Then Time' and 'Time and Materials' from *Time and Materials: Poems 1997–2005* by Robert Hass. Copyright © 2007 by Robert Hass. Reprinted by permission of HarperCollins Publishers. 'A Note on Metonymy' from *Twentieth Century Pleasures* by Robert Hass. Copyright © 1984 by Robert Hass. Reprinted by permission of HarperCollins Publishers.

JOHN MATTHIAS

'After Years Away', 'Rhododendron', 'Everything To Be Endured' and 'Not Having Read' from *Swimming at Midnight: Selected Shorter Poems* by John Matthias. Copyright © 1995 by John Matthias. Reprinted with the permission of Swallow Press/Ohio University Press, Athens, Ohio (www.ohioswallow.com). 'My Mother's Webster', 'Diminished Third', 'A Note on Barber's *Adagio*', 'Two in New York', 'Two in Harar' and 'Persistant Elegy' from *Pages: New Poems & Cuttings* by John Matthias. Copyright © 2000 by John Matthias. Reprinted with the permission of Swallow Press/Ohio University Press, Athens, Ohio (www.ohioswallow.com). 'She Maps Iraq' and 'Swell' from *New Selected Poems 1963–2003* by John Matthias. Copyright © 2004 by John Matthias. Reprinted by permission of Salt Publishing Ltd. 'Post-Anecdotal', 'Francophiles, 1958', 'Smultronstället', 'Four Seasons of Vladimir Dukelsky', 'Walter's House' and 'Tsunami: The Animals' from *Kedging: New Poems* by John Matthias. Copyright © 2007 by John Matthias. Reprinted by permission of Salt Publishing Ltd.

JAMES MCMICHAEL

Extract from 'Four Good Things' from *Four Good Things* (New York: Houghton Mifflin Harcourt, 1980). Copyright © 1980 by James McMichael. Extract from 'Each

Giroux, LLC. 'Book', 'Antique' from 'First Things to Hand', 'The Thicket', 'Veni, Creator Spiritus', 'In Defense of Allusion', 'Eurydice and Stalin', 'The Forgetting', 'Poem of Disconnected Parts', 'XYZ' and 'From the Last Canto of Paradise', from *Gulf Music* by Robert Pinsky. Copyright © 2007 by Robert Pinsky. Reprinted by permission of Farrar, Straus and Giroux, LLC. Extract from 'The Art of Poetry, no.76: Robert Pinsky', originally published in *The Paris Review*. Copyright © 1997 by The Paris Review, reprinted with permission of The Wylie Agency LLC.